GIVING
for All It's Worth

*Cultivating the grace of giving is vital
to a woman's relationship with God.*

D1512228

Gospel Advocate Company
1006 Elm Hill Pike
Nashville, Tennessee 37210

*Cultivating the grace of giving is vital
to a woman's relationship with God.*

GIVING
for All It's Worth

Melissa Lester

Scriptures, unless otherwise noted, taken from the NEW AMERICAN STANDARD BIBLE, ©1960, 1962, 1963, 1968, 1971, 1972, 1973, 1975, 1977 by The Lockman Foundation. Used by permission.

Published by Gospel Advocate Co.
1006 Elm Hill Pike, Nashville, TN 37210
www.gospeladvocate.com

ISBN: 0-89225-470-X

DEDICATION

For the women in my life who
have taught me the most about giving:
my mother, Sharon Prichard,
and my sister, Jennifer Driver

With deepest love and thanks to
my husband and best friend,
Joe

TABLE OF CONTENTS

FOREWORD

I still remember the confident young woman sitting across from me eight years ago. She was about to graduate from Lipscomb University and looking for a job. Even then she had specific career goals in mind – to work for *Christian Woman* magazine, to someday be editor of *Christian Woman*, to write books to teach and encourage women, and to become a speaker for women's retreats and special events. So far, Melissa Lester has achieved three of those goals.

For two years, Melissa used her editing and writing skills at the Gospel Advocate Co., which included working on *Christian Woman*. During that time, Melissa continued to cultivate the grace of giving that I'm sure was planted by her parents.

I remember how as newlyweds, Melissa and Joe helped a woman and her child who lived in the duplex next door. Believing the woman was being physically abused by her boyfriend, they reported the abuse to the proper authorities. The neighbor told Melissa that was the first time anyone had intervened on her behalf. The spiteful boyfriend had the woman's utilities turned off and left her with no income. Melissa and Joe offered baby-sitting services and financial assistance until the woman could get on her feet.

Another time, while dining at a local restaurant, Melissa and Joe encountered a waitress who was rude and inattentive. Rather than lash out at her, they decided she must be having a bad day and

would see what they could do to make it better. Melissa left her
a note of encouragement and a sizeable tip. Before they were able
to exit the restaurant, the waitress found them and tearfully
thanked them for the note and their generosity.

Today, Melissa continues to work with *Christian Woman* as a
contributing editor for the column "Creative Corner." She is a devoted wife and mother, a faithful servant, a gracious hostess and
a loyal friend. If anyone practices the grace of giving it is Melissa.
Perhaps her giving spirit will help you cultivate a giving spirit of
your own. I know she has planted a few seeds in my heart.

Debra G. Wright
Managing Editor
Christian Woman
June 2002

INTRODUCTION

Thank you for joining me for this study. We are embarking on a great adventure! On our journey through Scripture, we will encounter many fascinating women with much to teach us about giving. Many of these women you have met before, but I hope they will inspire you in new ways as we get to know them better.

Throughout our study, we must remember that these Bible heroines are not fictional characters. They were real women with real hopes and challenges. Most important, they were women whose choices demonstrated real faith.

With each woman we study, let us consider the world she lived in and the virtues she displayed. Think about her choices. Try to put yourself in her shoes. Chapters 2 through 11 begin with narratives intended to help you do this. These fictionalized accounts are included to help bring each character to life in your mind. As you imagine how she might have lived, perhaps you will find a mentor in a woman who lived long ago.

The narratives are not meant to replace or contradict biblical accounts. After each narrative, we will look to the Bible for the real story. There we will learn about each woman's service and make application to our lives. As we study together, may the grace of giving take root in your heart and spur you to greater service to God.

CHAPTER 1

THE GRACE OF GIVING

"But just as you excel in everything – in faith, in speech, in knowledge, in complete earnestness and in your love for us – see that you also excel in this grace of giving" (2 Corinthians 8:7 NIV).

Three-year-old Bridgette's blonde curls bobbed and her blue eyes sparkled as she watched her parents partake of the Lord's Supper. As the time drew near for the offering, she grew distracted waiting to deposit her shiny coins into the collection plate. As the men waiting on the table began making their way down the aisle, Bridgette's mother leaned over and whispered, "Bridgette, are you ready to give your money to God?"

With this, she popped to attention: "Yes! Which one is He?"

I can remember my own childhood enthusiasm as I waited to empty my beaded coin purse into the plate as it passed. I remember hearing members of the congregation being exhorted to "give of their means." "What does that mean?" my small mind wondered.

As an adult, I still believe this is an issue worth exploring. For the Christian, the commitment to give of our means goes beyond tithing and becomes life-encompassing. An attitude of generosity should permeate every aspect of our lives so that we may "excel in this grace of giving" (2 Corinthians 8:7).

Giving is to be done generously, lovingly and cheerfully (Matthew 10:8; 1 Corinthians 13:3; Psalm 37:21).

> Let each one do just as he has purposed in his heart; not grudgingly or under compulsion; for God loves a cheerful giver. And God is able to make all grace abound to you, that always having all sufficiency in everything, you

may have an abundance for every good deed (2 Corinthians 9:7-8).

God blesses each of us with unique opportunities in His kingdom. No matter our age, economic background, marital status, educational level or professional aptitude, we all have the ability to give. Many women of the Bible set powerful examples of giving that are still relevant today. We will look at several of them in our next 11 chapters. Each chapter begins with a narrative, which is designed to help you visualize these women and their choices more clearly. As we delve into Scripture, perhaps you will find your own potential mirrored in those of the women we study. Our strengths are multiplied when used for God's glory.

As we begin, let us look at why cultivating the grace of giving is so vital to our relationship with God.

We Are Commanded to Give

In the Sermon on the Mount, Jesus gave His followers a new mandate. Under the Old Law, concepts of giving were tempered by requirements for fairness. Jesus' listeners were familiar with the idea of "eye for eye, tooth for tooth" (Exodus 21:24). But in Matthew 25:38-42, Jesus urged them to return mercy for evil. He also told them to give freely to anyone who asks. Such selfless giving pleases our Lord.

Our willingness to give is a matter of eternal significance because we will be judged according to the way we serve others. Matthew 25:31-40 says Christ will separate the sheep from the goats. He will invite those on His right to enter the kingdom, praising them for attending to His needs. Perplexed, the faithful will ask when had they fed, sheltered or visited Him. Verse 40 tells us, "And the King will answer and say to them, 'Truly I say to you, to the extent that you did it to one of these brothers of Mine, even the least of them, you did it to Me.' "

At the heart of giving is obedience to God. As young Christians, giving may be done out of compulsion or a sense of duty. As we mature in our faith, however, our relationship with God grows and along with it our joy in serving others. Children obey their parents out of fear and respect in their youth, but as they mature, they desire to make decisions that will please and honor their parents because they love them. As God's children, we must trust His sovereignty and give freely as He directs. As our spirits become more generous, we will see more opportunities to give. We will feel privileged to serve because we want to delight our Father in heaven. When we do His will, our lives will be enriched, and much good will follow.

Giving to the Lord is easier when we realize that all that we have and all that we are already belong to Him. Psalm 50 declares God's supremacy and dominion over everything. Verses 9-14 assert,

> I shall take no young bull out of your house,
> Nor male goats out of your folds.
> For every beast of the forest is Mine,
> The cattle on a thousand hills.
> I know every bird of the mountains,
> And everything that moves in the field is Mine.
> If I were hungry, I would not tell you;
> For the world is Mine, and all it contains.
> Shall I eat the flesh of bulls,
> Or drink the blood of male goats?
> Offer to God a sacrifice of thanksgiving,
> And pay your vows to the Most High.

God does not ask us to give because He needs our sacrifices. The world and all that is in it are His. What we give to Him is already His, but our Father desires that we cultivate the grace of giving because He loves us. God graciously heaps blessings upon us, but with our blessings come responsibilities to serve Him. Good stewardship is an important concept to put into practice.

Giving Expresses Gratitude to God

David, a man after God's own heart, demonstrated a spirit of gratitude throughout his life. David's poetry in the book of Psalms is filled with passages brimming with praise and appreciation:

> I will praise you, O Lord, with all my heart;
> I will tell of all your wonders.
> I will be glad and rejoice in you;
> I will sing praise to your name, O Most High.
>
> (Psalm 9:1-2 NIV)

David recognized his indebtedness to God and was willing to pay a price to honor Him. Second Samuel 24:10-25 relates an interesting story in the life of David. The anger of the Lord was aroused against Israel, and God told King David's prophet, Gad, to offer the king three choices of punishment: seven years of famine, three months on the run from his enemies, or three days' plague.

A distressed David pleaded for mercy and asked that he not be delivered into the hands of man. For this reason, the Lord sent a plague upon Israel, killing 70,000 people. But when "the angel stretched out his hand over Jerusalem to destroy it, the Lord relented from the destruction, and said to the angel who was destroying the people, 'It is enough; now restrain your hand' " (v. 16 NKJV).

Gad instructed David to build an altar to the Lord on the threshing floor of Araunah the Jebusite, where the angel of the Lord was. Araunah offered his threshing floor, oxen and all that he had to David, but David refused. "Then the king said to Araunah, 'No, but I will surely buy it from you for a price; nor will I offer burnt offerings to the Lord my God with that which costs me nothing' " (v. 24 NKJV). David paid 50 shekels of silver for the oxen and threshing floor. There he built an altar and offered sacrifices to the Lord. As a result, the Lord heeded David's prayers and withdrew the plague from Israel.

David recognized that a sacrifice without cost was really no sacrifice at all. This is a lesson that most of us recognize in our daily living, yet we often fail to put it into practice in our spiritual lives. How many of us would point dinner guests to the trash can to dig through scraps of leftovers? None of us would even consider offering the crumbs that fall from the table to friends for dinner? Yet how many of us, when giving ourselves to the Most High God, offer Him the scraps and crumbs of our lives and resources? Our gratitude to God is reflected in the way we give to Him.

Our Giving Ministers to Those in Need

We find opportunities to give to souls in need every day. Our families, friends, co-workers, neighbors and acquaintances all face struggles and need encouragement from time to time. It is important for us to open our eyes to minister to the people we interact with throughout the day. Sometimes a smile or a kind word ministers greatly. As Proverbs 25:11 attests, "A word fitly spoken is like apples of gold In settings of silver" (NKJV). Many times we cannot fully know the impact of a small gesture of kindness. A brief phone call, a note of encouragement or well-timed hug might provide much-needed comfort to someone who needs to feel God's love in a tangible way.

Other times, our commitment to give must be greater. The good Samaritan of Luke 10 compassionately gave his time and resources to a stranger in need. In this parable, the Samaritan went out of his way to serve an unlikely neighbor. "Go and do likewise," Jesus urged in verse 37. Others besides the Samaritan passed by the injured man without stopping to investigate his condition. We must be watchful as we go through our hurried lives that we do not race by those who need our care.

God Is Glorified When We Give

The giving spirit of the church in Corinth exalted God. Their generosity helped people in need and resulted in thanksgiving to God. In 2 Corinthians 9:13, Paul wrote, "Because of the service by which you have proved yourselves, men will praise God for the obedience that accompanies your confession of the gospel of Christ" (NIV). When we give in the name of the Lord, we bring honor to the cause of Christ.

Even our smallest acts of kindness can bring great glory to God. To us, preparing a meal for someone in need may mean an extra trip to the grocery store, a few additional dollars spent on ingredients, and a couple of hours in the kitchen. But to a Christian sister who has just had a baby or who is recuperating from an illness, our small sacrifice means so much more. In addition to offering nourishment, the meal we provide is a touching reminder to her that she can depend on her heavenly Father and her church family to meet her needs in difficult times.

If we view our actions and attitudes in serving as a reflection on our Father, then we will be motivated to give. When we give as individuals, we honor the Lord; but when we give as a church family, our efforts are compounded even more in the glory they bring to God. The cause of Christ is strengthened when we purpose in our hearts to give.

Others Are Encouraged to Give as We Do

When we give generously and cheerfully, we influence other people to follow our example. Paul told the saints in Achaia,

> For I know your eagerness to help, and I have been boasting about it to the Macedonians, telling them that since last year you in Achaia were ready to give; and your enthusiasm has stirred most of them to action (2 Corinthians 9:2 NIV).

Both those who see our giving hearts and those who experience our generosity are encouraged to share their blessings as we do.

When most of us reflect on occasions of loss, sorrow or adversity, our dark memories are brightened by remembrances of the gracious expressions of comfort and kindness we received from God's people during those times. These loving acts of kindness motivate us to serve other people in similar circumstances.

Shortly after the birth of our first son, Joe and I faced the daunting prospect of moving. Joe's new job and daily three-hour commute kept him on the brink of exhaustion, and Carson's demanding infant schedule left me with no time to prepare. Worried about how we would manage the move, my mother related our plight to some Christian sisters at my home congregation. Two ladies immediately suggested that the three of them plan a trip to our home for a day of packing. This would mean seven hours of driving in one day for the two ladies, and Joe and I were at once honored and humbled that they would even consider such a sacrifice. Determined to help in any way they could, they brought my mother and spent a day cheerfully readying us for the move. Other Christian friends also helped us prepare. Joe and I still talk about the generosity we experienced during that trying time, and as a result we are encouraged to look for ways to lend a hand to others in need.

We Are Blessed When We Give

"In everything I did, I showed you that by this kind of hard work we must help the weak, remembering the words the Lord Jesus himself said: 'It is more blessed to give than to receive,'" Paul said in Acts 20:35 (NIV). With great struggle children learn to share their toys and reap the blessings of playing together. Many of us, however, never fully grow past our childish selfishness. How often does our heavenly Father gently prod us to open our clenched fists as our spirits defiantly stomp our feet and shout, "Mine!"? Even as we strive to teach our children to be generous, as adults we must diligently work to cultivate the grace of giving. Our joy, too, will be multiplied as we learn to share our blessings with those around us.

God smiles upon His children when we give. Luke 6:38 urges,

> Give, and it will be given to you. A good measure, pressed down, shaken together and running over, will be poured into your lap. For with the measure you use, it will be measured to you (NIV).

God rewards those who give generously. This was poignantly illustrated to my mother-in-law the summer she married. Betty traveled home by bus every weekend to work on wedding arrangements. One weekend, she had only $20 left when she went to church. She knew she needed the money for a bus ticket back to school, but she also needed to give to the Lord. She dropped the $20 in the collection plate when it passed. Later that day, a cousin stopped by and delivered a wedding gift: a crisp $20 bill.

Whenever we share our resources – whether our time, talents, money or other blessings – God sees our generous spirits and rewards us. Sometimes the blessings we receive are tangible, but many times the spiritual blessings He bestows on us are even greater. The Bible is filled with stories of people who excelled in the grace of giving and were blessed because of it. Among the examples of faithfulness, Abraham (Genesis 22:1-18; Hebrews 11:8-12, 17-19), Job (Job 1; 2:1-10; 42:10-17; James 5:11) and Noah (Genesis 6:5-22; Hebrews 11:7) made sacrifices in their obedience to God and were rewarded for their devotion. If we follow the biblical pattern, we, too, will find that it is more blessed to give than to receive.

For What It's Worth

There are many reasons to cultivate the grace of giving. In our study, we have explored six. We should give as a matter of obedience. Beyond this, we express our gratitude to God and glorify Him through our generosity. When we give, we help others and encourage them to follow our example. Finally, we reap blessings

when we give. When we give generously, cheerfully and lovingly, we fulfill the law of Christ. We all have unique strengths and
abilities to be used for God's purposes; therefore, we have varied
opportunities and responsibilities. Let us purpose in our hearts to
meet the daily challenge of giving of our means.

Give an Answer

1. Describe the attitudes God wants us to have when we give as
   described in 2 Corinthians 9:6-11.
2. Contrast Jesus' commands for selflessness in Matthew 5:38-42
   with the attitudes prevalent in our culture today.
3. How important is it for us to give (see Matthew 25:31-40)?
4. What important point does Psalm 50:7-15 bring out?
5. Relate the story of 2 Samuel 24:10-25. How important was
   David's attitude in God's decision to spare many lives in Israel?
6. How did the Achaians influence the Macedonians, according
   to Paul in 2 Corinthians 9:2?

Give It Some Thought

1. What does the phrase "the grace of giving" in 2 Corinthians
   8:7 mean to you?
2. List the six reasons to give that we explored in this chapter.
   Can you think of others?
3. How do our attitudes affect our opportunities to give?
4. Share an experience when you were surprised by generosity.
5. What part does sacrifice play in showing generosity? Why is it
   difficult to sacrifice?

Give It a Try

1. A key verse for this study will be 2 Corinthians 8:7. Commit it to
   memory or write it on a note and place it on your bathroom mir-
   ror to remind yourself daily to "excel in this grace of giving."
2. Send a note to someone whose generosity has blessed you and
   encouraged you to look for opportunities to serve.
3. Pray that during the weeks to come your eyes will be opened
   to opportunities to give of your means.

CHAPTER 2

PUTTING IN OUR TWO MITES WORTH

*"Let your character be free from the love of money, being
content with what you have; for He Himself has said,
'I will never desert you, nor will I ever forsake you,' so that
we confidently say, 'The Lord is my helper, I will not be afraid.
What shall man do to me?' " (Hebrews 13:5-6).*

The temple bustled with activity as people moved briskly in and out. The small widow slipped through the crowds quietly, careful to avoid the gaze of the scribes and Pharisees. A poor woman who came to the temple alone, she felt humbled in their presence. Their exquisitely detailed, flowing robes and jingling bags of money suggested an air of superiority. "How important they seem," she thought to herself. "They will certainly be long remembered."

As the widow made her way toward the treasury, a rich man brushed by her. Quickly she averted her eyes. As she instinctively looked toward the ground, her face flushed with embarrassment as she noticed the tattered edge of her own garment. Biting her lip, her palm felt damp as she tightened her grip on the two small copper coins she clutched. With a quick prayer of thanksgiving for God's mercy, she meekly placed the coins into the offering.

"I wish I could give more," she thought as she considered how God had sustained her since her husband's untimely death. Her heart still grieved for him, but God's love had been a balm for the agony of her loss. And although she could not boast riches, she had her health and the support of friends and relatives. Yes, God had been good to her. Praise His holy and blessed name.

As she turned to make her way out of the temple, her thoughts were interrupted by voices. A scribe was praying aloud nearby. His words were eloquent, his gestures dramatic. "Surely God will hear this devout man," she thought as she considered her own meager offering of praise.

A crowd had gathered in the distance to hear the Teacher she had seen in the temple on several occasions. She knew from the posture of the scribes and Pharisees surrounding Him that they did not approve of His teachings. Everyone knew that the scribes and Pharisees were learned men who could easily ensnare lesser students of Scripture in a debate. "How I wish that I could teach," she thought. "What greater goal could one pursue than to glorify God and encourage others to draw closer to Him?" And with a prayer on her heart and a final glimpse in the direction of the Teacher, she stepped out from the temple to face another day.

When asked to think of a woman in the Bible who exemplifies giving, your mind probably first goes back to the temple where Jesus sat teaching His disciples in the first four verses of Luke 21. In this brief passage, Christ was able to teach volumes about giving:

> And He looked up and saw the rich putting their gifts into the treasury. And He saw a certain poor widow putting in two small copper coins. And He said, "Truly I say to you, this poor widow put in more than all of them; for they all out of their surplus put into the offering; but she out of her poverty put in all that she had to live on" (vv. 1-4).

The widow in the temple gave two mites, a small amount by any standard. A mite was the smallest denomination of Jewish currency in that day, worth less than our penny. When the offerings were counted for that day, her two mites would hardly have been noticed. It was such an insignificant sum by earthly standards that many would have reasoned it was not even worth giving.

God's standards are not ours, however. Although the widow's offering was small in earthly value, its spiritual value was great because it was all that she had. She had no husband to depend on for financial strength. For a woman of her time and circumstances to make such a sacrifice demonstrates great faith in God. She truly gave all that she had to give.

Her attitude in making her offering pleased God. Although Scripture does not reveal whether she counted the cost or wondered about her future security before making her offering, we do see the depth of her faith revealed in her actions. She gave with an attitude of generosity, trust and humility. While the wealthy people in the temple that day noisily presented their offerings with great fanfare, she meekly deposited her feeble sum into the treasury.

This destitute woman is held up for us as an example of how we should give. Her actions modeled great faith and a proper attitude. She could never have imagined what a great lesson she taught in the temple that day or the long-reaching influence she would have. Her sacrifice was so great that the Son of God noticed her, Scripture records her story in Mark and Luke, and thousands of years later we are still talking about her. In *All of the Women of the Bible*, Edith Deen wrote,

> The cash value of her gift compared to the gifts of the wealthy was hardly enough to notice, but the devotion behind it was another matter. That devotion, beginning there and spreading throughout the world, has built hospitals and helped the needy, fed the hungry and encouraged the imprisoned. Today the world knows more about the poor widow than about the richest man in Jerusalem in her day (Harper Collins, New York, 1955; p. 353).

This widow provides a powerful example of giving money. God has given us further guidance about how to handle our material blessings. Other examples abound throughout the Bible to teach us how to give. Much good can come from our money when used to the glory of God. Let us look now to Scripture to learn more about the attitudes we are to have about money and our other physical blessings. We should all desire to be good stewards of what God has given us.

Money Is Neither Good Nor Evil

Many Christians have the notion that money is inherently evil, but that is not what the Bible teaches. First Timothy 6:10 cautions, "For the love of money is a root of all sorts of evil." This passage says that love of money, not money itself, is the root of evil. Money itself is morally neutral; when it reaches our hands it becomes good or bad. As Christians, we have a duty to work honestly and to provide financial support for our families (Romans 4:4; Colossians 3:23; 2 Thessalonians 3:10). If it is fairly earned and wisely used, money can be a tool for good. However, it can tempt people away from godliness into vain pursuits. Money can bring corruption in the hands of the greedy and unwise; but it has tremendous ability to bless people and spread God's love when used for His purposes.

We can see money being used throughout Scripture for positive and negative purposes. Listed here are a few instances where money was used for evil.

• Joseph's brothers sold him into slavery for 20 shekels of silver (Genesis 37:28).

• Achan stole 200 shekels of silver and a bar of gold 50 shekels in weight from the spoils of battle and buried it underneath his tent. The lives of Israelite soldiers were lost because of his greed, and ultimately it cost him his life and the lives of his family (Joshua 7:20-25).

• Judas betrayed Jesus for 30 pieces of silver (Matthew 26:14-16, 47-50).

Money was also used for good, as these passages indicate.

• The virtuous woman of Proverbs 31 wisely conducted business and invested her money for the benefit of her household (v. 16).

• In the parable of the good Samaritan, the Samaritan offered to pay whatever was required for the care of the injured man (Luke 10:30-35).

• The church at Corinth's liberality in giving cared for the saints, allowed Paul to minister more effectively, and helped spread the Gospel (2 Corinthians 9:12-15).

Still today money can bless or condemn us. If we heed the Bible's advice, we can avoid being tempted into evil by money.

Money Should Not Be Our Focus

Money is a matter of first importance for many people in our society. Second Timothy 3:2 begins, "For men will be lovers of self, lovers of money." This passage still rings true today. Notice the order of priorities for the worldly person: self first, riches second. Noticeably absent from this list are God, the church, family and people in need. People with this type of attitude believe that money is the ultimate source of happiness and fulfillment. Yet, like the prodigal son who squandered his fortune in riotous living in Luke 15, many people throughout history have found that a money-first attitude results in an empty, wasted life. Seeking riches to the detriment of all else will leave one spiritually bankrupt.

Great wealth can make people take their focus off of God, believing that they no longer need Him. Jesus told His disciples in Mark 10:25, "It is easier for a camel to go through the eye of a needle than for a rich man to enter the kingdom of God." Money can be a tremendous blessing, but we must always realize that all good things come from God and that we are lost without Him. We cannot maintain a dual focus on riches and God; God must be first.

"No servant can serve two masters; for either he will hate the one, and love the other, or else he will hold to one, and despise the other. You cannot serve God and mammon." Now the Pharisees, who were lovers of money, were listening to all these things, and they were scoffing at Him. And He said to them, "You are those who justify yourselves in the sight of men, but God knows your hearts; for that which is highly esteemed among men is detestable in the sight of God" (Luke 16:13-15).

God knows what is first in our hearts.

As Christians, most of us recognize that the pursuit of money should not be our first priority, yet we have not been able to escape its grasp on our hearts. Because we need money for food, clothing and shelter in our daily living, we let financial issues weigh heavily on our minds. Looking toward the future, we see looming financial obligations and grow distressed. A fretful focus on money can be just as spiritually damaging as a hedonistic focus on riches. When our hearts are filled with anxiety over money, where are we putting our trust? And how can we joyfully share with others when we feel burdened by our own concerns about money? Christ urges us in Matthew 6:26-34 to give our worries over to God and to put our trust in Him to provide for us.

Money Cannot Buy Spirituality

It is true that money cannot buy everything. In fact, it won't get you very far at all in the kingdom of God. Many people mistakenly believe that they can buy spiritual significance. Acts 8:18-24 relates a story that proves that God cannot be bought. When Simon saw that through the laying on of the apostles' hands, the Spirit was bestowed, he offered money in exchange for receiving the Holy Spirit. Peter was swift and harsh in his rebuke of Simon: "May your silver perish with you, because you thought you could obtain the gift of God with money!" (v. 20). Peter said Simon's heart was not right and urged him to repent.

Great wealth can give people the false hope that their spirituality is secure. "I am so blessed with riches," they reason, "God must be pleased with me." This is a dangerous philosophy because physical wealth and spiritual wealth do not necessarily correlate. Luke 12:15-21 warns against greed and cautions that life does not consist in an abundance of things. Christ told a parable in this passage of a man who tore down his old barns and built bigger ones to house his surplus of crops. He found solace in his earthly riches and purposed to eat, drink and be merry. However, the man died that night. God called him a fool for laying up treasures for himself without being "rich toward God" (v. 21). This foolish man put his trust in riches rather than God and paid the price in the end.

It is true that our salvation comes with a price, but that price was paid by Christ in His death on the cross. We cannot buy our way into God's grace with money or earthly riches. Although God wants us to demonstrate generosity with our earthly resources, it is not ultimately our money that He desires, but our hearts.

Rich or Poor, All Can Give

The beauty of the story of the widow who gave her two mites is in its clear demonstration that all can give. It is tempting to believe that only the rich have the responsibility to give, but the problem with that philosophy is that most of us probably wouldn't describe ourselves as rich. It is often easier to compare our station in life to those around us rather than looking at our own blessings. We can only purpose to give for ourselves, though, so judging other people's ability to give is fruitless. In Luke 3:7-11, Christ commanded all His followers to give. "Let the man who has two tunics share with him who has none; and let him who has food do likewise," he urged in verse 11. Most of us are rich indeed by those standards.

Giving financially might be an idea that we relish, yet we see it as something we will do down the road when we have reached financial security. You may have thought to yourself from time to time, "If I had a million dollars, I would love to contribute to Christian education." If you had a great sum of money, would you make donations to a mission effort, a children's home, your church library or some other worthy cause? If you would desire to give to a cause if you were rich, then why not give to it now? Perhaps you don't have a million dollars, but do you have $100? $10? $1? We all have some amount to give.

We assume sometimes that it would be easier to give of our riches, but that is not necessarily true. Suppose a very rich man offered to give you a dollar at a time until you had all the money you wanted. When would you have enough and tell him to stop? Most of us would probably gleefully keep our hands outstretched as long as we physically could. We may never reach the pinnacle of financial freedom that we are striving for, so we must train ourselves to give all along. Rather than waiting for riches before we decide to become charitable, we must cultivate the grace of giving with whatever amount we are blessed to have.

If we want to compare our blessings to anyone, let us look to those who have less than us. Many people go to bed hungry and homeless. How rich most of us would seem to these people! Let us not forget the poor widow who gave all she had in the temple. If out of her poverty she could give so much, then surely we can give too.

Our Attitude Is Important

The condition of our hearts is the most important aspect of giving. The Bible has given several guidelines about what our attitudes must be to please God.

We should not give with ourselves in mind. First Timothy 6:5 cautions against false teachers "who suppose that godliness is a means of gain." We should never give in order to receive blessings or to bring glory to ourselves. Our giving should be done with compassion toward those who need our money and in a way that brings honor to God.

We must be content with what we have. "But godliness actually is a means of great gain, when accompanied by contentment. For we have brought nothing into the world, so we cannot take anything out of it either. And if we have food and covering, with these we shall be content," 1 Timothy 6:6-8 continues. If we are satisfied with what we have, we will feel free to give to others. We will also save ourselves worry and financial strain because we will not try to live above our means.

We must give honestly. God knows our hearts, and we cannot lie to Him. The story of Ananias and Sapphira comes to mind to illustrate this point. In Acts 5:1-11, this couple sold a piece of property and secretly decided to keep back some of the profits for themselves. Looking for glory, they took a portion of the money to the apostles and lied about the selling price of the land. Both Ananias and Sapphira were struck dead and buried that day. The penalty they paid for their deception was hardly worth the money they attempted to hold back from the Lord.

We should give generously. Ephesians 5:3 urges us not to "let ... greed even be named among you, as is proper among saints." Christians should have the reputation of being generous and compassionate with their resources. As individuals, families and congregations, it is important that we cultivate a spirit of benevolence. As Christian women, we must look for opportunities to give and model generosity to our children.

Our giving should be discreet. "Beware of practicing your righteousness before men to be noticed by them; otherwise you have no reward with your Father who is in heaven" (Matthew 6:1). Although this point might seem to be at odds with earning a reputation of generosity, it really is not. The grace of giving will be evident to people around us if we practice it, but we should not draw attention to our giving. We should give discreetly so that we may glorify God.

Our Blessings Bring Responsibility

In the parable of the talents in Matthew 25:14-30, the master gave five talents to one servant, two to another, and one to the last. A long time later when the master returned, he found that the man to whom he had given five talents had gained five more and the man to whom he had entrusted two talents had gained two more. The master had praise and more responsibility for these two servants who had doubled their talents. "Well done, good and faithful slave; you were faithful with a few things, I will put you in charge of many things; enter into the joy of your master," he told each servant in verses 21 and 23.

The servant who had received one talent did not please his master, though, for he buried the talent in the ground. The master chastised him and gave his talent to the servant with 10 talents. The parable is summed up in Luke 25:29, "For to everyone who has shall more be given, and he shall have an abundance; but from the one who does not have, even what he does have shall be taken away." It is important that we become good stewards of all that God has entrusted to us. Just as the servants in the parable realized that the talents belonged to their master, so should we realize that our material blessings belong to our Master.

To whom much is given, much is expected. According to Luke 16:10-11, "He who is faithful in a very little thing is faithful also in much; and he who is unrighteous in a very little thing is unrighteous also in much. If therefore you have not been faithful in the use of unrighteous mammon, who will entrust the true riches to you?" Along with our blessings from God come additional responsibilities to serve.

We Must Be Willing to Give What Is Needed

The rich young ruler of Mark 10 asked Jesus what he must do to inherit eternal life. He felt secure in his obedience to the commandments but was saddened to hear Jesus' answer: "One thing you lack: go and sell all you possess, and give to the poor, and you shall have treasure in heaven; and come, follow me" (v. 21). Christ's answer humbled the young man, who probably had been looking for validation of his faithfulness. Instead his heart was pricked and he went away sorrowful. Although this ruler had kept the commandments from his youth, he lacked the sacrificial attitude that God desires.

God joyfully blesses us and does not literally ask us all to sell

everything that we have. We must be willing to give what is needed, however. If we are to give sacrificially, this will not happen without our commitment. Nearing the end of my college career, classmates and I were asked to prepare post-graduation budgets for a
financial planning course. My professor was disheartened when
most of us forgot to include planned giving to the local church in
our budgets. She stressed to us the importance of establishing a
discipline of giving early on in our independence. Her words have
stuck with me and remind me that giving is a decision. We must
purpose in our hearts to give to God first, not last. Planned giving is an important first step toward giving in a way that will please
and glorify our Lord.

For What It's Worth

Money can be a tool for good or a barrier between us and righteousness. If we purpose in our hearts to give like the widow who
gave her two mites, our money will be a tremendous blessing.
We are to give generously, compassionately, honestly and discreetly to meet the needs of those around us and to glorify God.
To whom much has been given, much is expected. But whether
rich or poor, we all have something to give. We must never be so
attached to our material blessings that they build a partition between us and God. We must remember that all that we have belongs to God and that we are stewards of what is already His.
Keeping that in mind, we will be able to give what He asks with
a generous and cheerful heart.

Give an Answer

1. Share biblical examples that illustrate money being used for
   good or evil.
2. Recall the story of Simon in Acts 8:18-24. How was Simon's
   thinking flawed?
3. What command did Christ give His followers in Luke 3:11?
4. Describe the attitude God expects when we give as taught in
   the Bible.
5. According to Luke 16:10-11, how will we be entrusted with
   great riches?

6. Contrast the focus of the worldly person as described in 2 Timothy 3:2 with that of the Christian.

Give It Some Thought

1. What do you believe are the greatest lessons to be learned from the widow who gave her two mites?
2. Why is it so difficult not to focus on money? How can we avoid being hedonistic or fretful?
3. What can we learn from the rich young ruler of Mark 10?
4. What excuses do we sometimes use for not giving?
5. Why is it important to make a conscious decision to give?

Give It a Try

1. Have you made a commitment to give? Prepare a budget, and look for ways you can increase your planned giving.
2. If you give your children an allowance, teach them to give first to God. Encourage their generous spirits when they want to support good works.
3. Make an anonymous donation to someone in need, or give to a worthy cause in the name of your congregation.

CHAPTER 3

GIVING
OUR GIFTS

*"And since we have gifts that differ according to the grace given
to us, let each exercise them accordingly" (Romans 12:6).*

F ar off in the distance, as if in a dream, she heard Peter's voice:
"Tabitha, arise."

Opening her eyes, she saw that it was not a dream, for there was
Peter before her. "What a dear man of God. He did come, after all,"
she thought. She had been so weak and tired lately, not quite herself. As she grew sicker by the day, quietly within her heart she
had hoped that Peter would come. Of course, she would never have
expected him to travel to Joppa. "He is busy doing the Lord's work,"
she had reminded herself. "He should not be bothered to help such
a lowly servant as me."

Dorcas, as she was usually called, rarely succumbed to illness,
but recent dizzy spells and trembling fingers had left her unable to
tend to those who needed her. A capable seamstress, she delight-
ed in making clothing for the poor. She had learned to sew at her
mother's knee and since her youth used her skills to minister to
the needy. With each careful stitch, she would hum praises to the
Lord or offer quiet prayers for the widows she helped clothe. When
she grew ill, it had pained her to put down her needle and thread.

Peter smiled gently and extended his hand. On her feet again for
the first time, she felt steady. How wonderful it felt to breathe deeply
and freely. She squeezed Peter's hand and returned his smile.
"Thank you," she whispered. "And thank You, Almighty God," she
prayed silently.

Muffled sounds from downstairs drew her attention. As Peter opened the door, she heard anguished voices. Peter called to the saints and widows to come in. As they ascended the stairs, sounds of weeping gave way to jubilant cries. Those who had been huddled together in sorrow now rushed to her side, tears still wet on their cheeks. Their joyful embraces one after another nearly left her breathless.

As the afternoon sun began to fade, the crowd dwindled until at last she was alone. Pausing to drink in the tranquility this solitude brought, she surveyed the room before her. Her eyes came to rest on the crumpled fabric in the corner. Before she had taken ill, she had been working on a cloak for one of the older widows in Joppa. Illness had forced her to push the project aside, but the heap of cloth now seemed to beckon her.

She smiled contentedly as she crossed the room to gather her needle and thread. Cooler weather was on its way, after all, and she had work to do before the sun set on this day.

Acts 9:36-42 relates the inspiring story of Tabitha, or Dorcas, a woman who "was full of good works and charitable deeds which she did" (v. 36 NKJV). She was well known and greatly loved for her willingness to serve. When she became ill and died, the saints washed her body and laid her in an upper room. Two men travelled to Lydda, which was near her hometown of Joppa, to find Peter. Peter arrived in Joppa to find a grieving crowd in the upper room. "And all the widows stood by him weeping, showing the tunics and garments which Dorcas had made while she was with them," according to verse 39. Because of her faithfulness and the power of God, Dorcas was restored to life by Peter. This miraculous healing encouraged the saints and helped spread the good news, as verse 42 attests: "And it became known throughout all Joppa, and many believed on the Lord" (NKJV).

What an example we have in Dorcas! She was a woman who used her talents to glorify God, and Scripture records the tremendous impact she had on the people she served. As a seamstress, she did more than meet the physical needs of the impoverished people she assisted. Besides keeping them warm, dry and clothed, the garments Dorcas made ministered to the widows by giving them tangible proof that they had not been forgotten. Each stitch signified her concern for them, and her careful work showed them that they were worthy of her attention. In a time when they could have felt lost and alone, Dorcas' attentiveness to their needs must have made them feel validated and appreciated. Ultimately, through her good works she demonstrated the love of God. With needle and thread, she crafted garments and ministered to the people around her.

The example of Dorcas shows us what God can accomplish when we are willing to give Him our hearts and our hands. He can do great things when we are willing to use our gifts and abilities to His glory. What a privilege it is to think that we can serve as vessels through which others can see and experience the love of Christ. The Lord has blessed each of us with unique potential to serve in the kingdom, and it is exciting to consider the possibilities before us.

One of a Kind

With great care God created us individually, as Psalm 139:13-16 recognizes. Verses 13-14 say, "For Thou didst form my inward parts; Thou didst weave me in my mother's womb. I will give thanks to Thee, for I am fearfully and wonderfully made." It is awe-inspiring to realize that no two people who have ever walked the earth are exactly alike. We are all special, individual and peculiar – all molded by the hand of God. How remarkable it is to consider that the Creator of the universe made each of us exclusively. Each of us is truly one of a kind.

For this reason, we rejoice each time a new soul is brought into the world. With great anticipation we look forward to the birth of a child to see how the magnificent handiwork of God will manifest itself anew. Many hours of pregnancy are spent wondering about the baby who is developing day by day. Who will she look like? Will his eyes be green or brown? Will she be bubbly and extroverted or introverted and reflective? Will he write poetry, love painting or be a star athlete? Will she play the piano, love gardening or be a culinary genius? Our Father knows all this and more. He knows every detail about us, down to the number of hairs on our heads (Matthew 10:30; Luke 12:7).

As babes in Christ, it is exciting to consider the opportunities the Lord has in store for each of us. Our Father, who lovingly created us, has blessed us all with unique gifts that can be used for His glory. As we grow to maturity in Christ, we will find new opportunities to share our gifts with those around us. As individuals with distinctive personalities and varied abilities, each of us will have unique opportunities to serve and to share.

In this chapter, the challenge before you is to evaluate your potential to excel in the discipline of giving in new ways. Our focus will principally center on these areas for personal reflection:

Talents: Webster defines talent as "innate mental or artistic aptitude (as opposed to acquired ability)." Talents are general areas of natural ability that may be further cultivated through study or practice.

Skills: According to the dictionary, a skill is the "ability to do something well, especially as the result of long practical experience" or "a particular technique." These abilities are acquired through life experience, education or professional training.

Interests: Among Webster's definitions of the word "interest" are "curiosity about, or intellectual or emotional involvement in something" and "something on which these feelings are fixed." Taking a look at our interests might reveal talents that are as yet unexplored.

"What would you like to be when you grow up?" we often ask children. We delight in learning about their latest dreams as well as what these future plans reveal about their burgeoning self-awareness. Most of us realize the importance of nurturing children and encouraging them to reach their full potential, but as adults we may have neglected to fulfill our own promise. With open hearts and a willingness to give of our abilities, however, we can impact the lives of those around us. Each of us has a unique role to play in the kingdom if we are willing. As we delve into this study, examine your talents, skills and interests. Perhaps you will find new opportunities to cultivate the grace that comes from giving in your life.

We All Have Gifts

Perhaps you are already eager to move on to the next chapter, sure that you don't have any unique gifts to offer. How mistaken that attitude is! God lovingly created each of us with a unique potential to make a difference in the lives of those around us. First Corinthians 12:4-11 deals with spiritual gifts, but the passage also has broader application for our study. Verses 4 through 7 show that our gifts come from God:

> Now there are varieties of gifts, but the same Spirit. And there are varieties of ministries, and the same Lord. And there are varieties of effects, but the same God who works all things in all persons. But to each one is given the manifestation of the Spirit for the common good.

Verses 8 through 10 list spiritual gifts, and verse 11 sums up the passage: "But one and the same Spirit works all these things, distributing to each one individually just as He wills."

Although our focus in this lesson is not necessarily on spiritual gifts, this is still an important passage for our study because it shows us several key points. First, it acknowledges that God is our Creator and the Giver of our gifts. He has blessed all of us, the passage points out, and therefore deserves the credit for our talents. Second, we see that we are uniquely blessed. We don't all have the same abilities, desires or interests. This is as God intended because just as our talents are varied, our responsibilities will be different. And third, our gifts are purposefully given by God for the good of those around us. We are expected to use our resources to glorify God and serve others.

Dorcas in the Modern Day

As Christian women, there is so much that we can do in the kingdom of God. Although the Bible does not give us examples of women leading in worship, its pages are filled with women whose godly lives helped lead people to the Lord. Dorcas is a prime example of someone who used her talents to bring glory to God. She effectively used her abilities to minister to those in need and to demonstrate God's love.

I have been blessed to know many modern-day Dorcases whose

talents, skills and interests have been used, with joy and creativity, to minister to others and spread God's love. Their examples exhort me to look for opportunities to serve in my own life. Listed here are just a few of the many women who have taught me about the blessings that come from learning to give.

• Sandra Humphrey of Oakhurst, Calif., author and editor of *Christian Woman* magazine, uses her writing ability to spread the good news and encourage Christian women in their daily walk with God.

• Jennifer Kachelman of Memphis, Tenn., is blessed with tremendous creative talent, which is well matched by her generous spirit. She is a gifted cook, seamstress and crafter who delights in teaching other sisters as well as making gifts for them.

• Nurse Connie Robbins of Morristown, Tenn., compassionately combines medical knowledge with empathy and understanding to offer support and advice to church members struggling with illness.

• Carole Purkey of Nashville, Tenn., uses her organizational abilities and people skills to direct weddings, plan ladies retreats and work in a variety of ministries.

• Lynn Ellis of Enterprise, Ala., works tirelessly each summer alongside her husband, Keith, at Wiregrass Christian Youth Camp. A thoughtful and wise counselor, she uses her interest in music to bond with like-minded young people.

• My mother, Sharon Prichard, and sister, Jennifer Driver, have the gift of encouragement. Both use their listening skills and nurturing instincts to minister in their work: Mother as secretary for the church in Morristown, Tenn., and Jennifer as head resident of a women's dorm at Lipscomb University in Nashville.

• My grandmother, Frances Prichard, of Jacksonville, Ala., spent many hours teaching me to paint, sew and embroider as I was growing up. In our special times together, she helped cultivate my interest in crafting.

How can you put your unique gifts to use to be a modern-day Dorcas? Perhaps your athletic ability or computer savvy could offer an opportunity to teach and mentor young people. Or maybe your church bulletin boards or classrooms would benefit from your artistic touch. If you work as a lawyer, financial planner or counselor, do you seek opportunities to help those less fortunate? Look at your talents, professional skills and hobbies as tools to serve God, and you will be amazed at the opportunities that will come your way.

All God's Gifts Are Good

We sometimes feel intimidated when observing the talents of those around us rather than focusing on developing our own abilities. Envy and self-doubt can creep in when we consider other people's gifts more important than our own, but such an attitude is not pleasing to God. One talent is not superior to another, and it takes a diversity of gifts to fulfill a variety of needs in the church. As 1 Corinthians 12:14-19 points out, the body comprises many members, all of which are necessary. Just as our physical bodies require the cooperation of many organs, the church needs the work of all its members. Rather than feeling disheartened by areas where we lack talent, we should appreciate the abilities of other Christians and strive to improve our own. Our gifts are all good because they come from a good and wise God.

There is no room for insecurity, jealousy or competition in the kingdom of God. We have far too much work to do, and it will take the whole body working together to be productive. As members of the body, we should recognize and show our appreciation for the roles played by other members. Our edification of one another can motivate us to use our talents, skills and interests for the good of the kingdom. When we work together to use our gifts in the body, we will be "joined and knit together by what every joint supplies," according to Ephesians 4:16 (NKJV), which will cause "growth of the body for the edifying of itself in love."

Giving Our Talents to God

It is common in today's religious world for people to seek to use their talents in worship to God. Although many of these well-meaning people sincerely want to please God and believe that they are glorifying Him, there are several problems with their philosophy. First, the focus of such worship is only on entertainment-oriented talents. Christians blessed with musical or dramatic abilities may be eager to share their talents in corporate worship, but what about the gifted mathematician, star athlete or renowned chef? If God really desires us to bring our unique talents to worship, then should-n't we all contribute equally? It would not be practical or reasonable for this to be done "decently and in order," as 1 Corinthians 14:40 (NKJV) says our worship should be.

A second problem with this philosophy is that it puts people in leadership roles in worship whose preparation may not even include Bible study or spiritual development. It would be possible for these talented people to achieve an elevated status in the congregation when in fact they might not even be committed believers. How could we think that this might be pleasing to God?

The third problem with this philosophy is that it places the focus of worship on man, rather than on God. Second Timothy 4:3 warns against those who want to have their ears tickled in worship. We must remember that our worship is for God, not ourselves. If it is done in accordance with His will, Christians will be edified and strengthened in worship. Our own preferences and tastes should not be the first priority, however. Because God has told us the elements that He wants in corporate worship, who are we to decide that He has changed His mind?

Finally, applying our unique talents to corporate worship may seem like an enlightened idea, but it is really limiting. We spend only a few hours a week worshiping God as a church body. Instead of trying to squeeze our talents into corporate worship, why not worship God during those hours as He directs and focus our attention on using our talents to His glory in our lives? Certainly God expects us to use our talents in a way that honors Him, but our Christianity is to be life-permeating and evident beyond the few hours a week we gather at the church building. Rather than focusing solely on giving ourselves to God in worship, let us seek to give our whole lives to God in accordance with Romans 6:13, which urges us to "present yourselves to God as those alive from the dead, and your members as instruments of righteousness to God."

Putting Talent to Good Use

If our giving is to be life-permeating, we must strive to use all of the resources at our disposal to the glory of God. The Bible has given us some guidance as to how we are to use our gifts and abilities to please God.

We should do everything to the best of our ability.

> Whatever you do, do your work heartily, as for the Lord
> rather than for men; knowing that from the Lord you will
> receive the reward of the inheritance. It is the Lord Christ
> whom you serve (Colossians 3:23-24).

We must look for opportunities to serve.

> And let us not lose heart in doing good, for in due time
> we shall reap if we do not grow weary. So then, while we
> have opportunity, let us do good to all men, and espe-
> cially to those who are of the household of the faith
> (Galatians 6:9-10).

We must have the proper attitude.

> Do all things without grumbling or disputing; that you
> may prove yourselves to be blameless and innocent, chil-
> dren of God above reproach in the midst of a crooked
> and perverse generation, among whom you appear as
> lights in the world (Philippians 2:14-15).

We must give God the glory for our abilities.

> I am the vine, you are the branches; he who abides in
> Me, and I in him, he bears much fruit; for apart from Me
> you can do nothing (John 15:5).

We should use our gifts in a way that brings honor to God.

> Let your light so shine before men, that they may see
> your good works and glorify your Father in heaven
> (Matthew 5:16 NKJV).

For What It's Worth

Within each of us are God-given gifts that are to be used to His
glory. If we develop the proper attitude in serving, our talents, skills
and interests can become tools to minister to those around us. We
must evaluate our unique abilities, work to develop them, and seek
opportunities to use them to honor our Father. If we are willing to
offer our hearts and hands in service to God, then like Dorcas, we
can be vessels of the love of God.

Give an Answer

1. Relate the story of Dorcas as told in Acts 9:36-42.
2. How are we made according to Psalm 139:13-16?
3. List three key points we can take from 1 Corinthians 12:4-11.
4. How do our unique abilities impact the kingdom as described in 1 Corinthians 12:14-25?
5. Read Matthew 5:13-16. What does this passage reveal about what our attitudes should be in sharing our gifts?
6. Of what important point does John 15:4-5 remind us?

Give It Some Thought

1. Why do you think Dorcas was so beloved by the widows and saints?
2. Who are some modern-day Dorcases in your congregation?
3. How have you been blessed by the unique abilities of a Christian sister?
4. What are the pitfalls of comparing our gifts to those of our sisters in Christ?
5. What blessings come from using our talents to glorify God?

Give It a Try

1. List your talents, skills and interests in the left-hand column of a piece of paper. In the right-hand column, brainstorm ideas for using these gifts to minister to others.
2. Think back to a pastime of your youth. Consider rekindling an interest in this hobby and exploring the opportunities for service it brings.
3. Take a class, read a book or devote time to strengthening your prowess in an area where you can use your abilities to the glory of God.

CHAPTER 4

THE GRACIOUS HOSTESS

"Be hospitable to one another without complaint" (1 Peter 4:9).

"**M**y, how life has changed," Lydia mused as she busied herself with last-minute preparations. Paul, Silas and the other saints would be arriving soon, and she wanted to have ready a warm and comfortable refuge for her guests after the drama that had surrounded the past few days. It seemed only yesterday that she had met Paul and Silas on the riverbank and had heard them proclaim the good news of Jesus Christ. After she and her household were baptized, she had urged them to come to her home. Little did she know then what was to befall these men of God in the days to come.

As she swept the floor and tidied her house, Lydia was deep in thought. She could hardly believe the events that had unfolded since her recent conversion. Just days after she had accepted the gospel, Paul and Silas were seized in the marketplace and dragged before the magistrates. There the apostles had been falsely charged, stripped, beaten and thrown into prison. Lydia shuddered with horror as she considered the agony that her new brothers in Christ had endured at the hands of her fellow citizens.

The aroma of freshly baked bread called Lydia back to the present. Paul and Silas were being released from prison today, and she was certain they would be hungry and tired when they arrived. Their wounds would need to be tended, as well. Other Christians would be coming, eager to hear the apostles' encouraging tales of God's providential care. Lydia was happy knowing that her home would be filled with the joyful sounds of praise to God. "Please let me use this home in a way that will please and glorify You," she prayed.

Sounds of approaching footsteps and rising voices outside alerted Lydia that guests were near. "Father, please help me offer respite to these men of God, and open my eyes to ways that I may minister to their needs," Lydia pleaded in a final silent prayer. Then, smiling widely, she opened her front door and extended her hand to welcome God's servants into her home and into her heart.

In the story of Lydia, as told in Acts 16:11-40, we see the impact a woman of God can have when she opens her home to those in need. Lydia, a seller of purple from Thyatira, was converted by Paul on the bank of a river outside Philippi. She had gathered with other women to pray on the Sabbath, as was her custom, and there she heard the gospel. "The Lord opened her heart to heed the things spoken by Paul," verse 14 (NKJV) says. After she and all her household were baptized, she entreated Paul and Silas, "If you have judged me to be faithful to the Lord, come to my house and stay" (v. 15 NKJV). Paul and Silas were persuaded to accept her invitation. Later, after Paul and Silas were beaten, cast into prison and then released, they went straight to Lydia's home where they were welcomed by Lydia and other brethren.

Upon accepting the good news of Christ, Lydia immediately extended her hand in hospitality. No doubt, she could have excused herself from giving in this way for many reasons. First, as a businesswoman, her schedule was probably already quite full. House guests would certainly have made her too busy. Second, she had just met Paul and Silas. Surely there were other people who knew them better who could house them. And finally, after the frightening scene that took place in the marketplace, Lydia could have feared for her safety. She might put herself and her household at risk by taking in these controversial men.

Instead of offering excuses, however, Lydia welcomed Paul and Silas into her home with graciousness. How comforting it must have been to them while in prison to know that a haven awaited them upon their release. Lydia must have been known for her hospitality, because other Christians knew to go to her home also. Her house was surely a refuge for the saints who gathered together to pray for the safe deliverance of Paul and Silas. By offering to share her home, Lydia offered comfort, support and security to the apostles and her fellow Christians.

Lydia must have been the type of person to whom people are drawn and with whom they feel at ease. She was certainly among the Christians to whom Paul later addressed the epistle to the Philippians. Philippians 1:3 reads, "I thank my God upon every remembrance of you" (NKJV). Through practicing hospitality like Lydia, we may minister to lost souls, encourage the saints, and develop friendships that will sustain us throughout life.

A Place for Us

For those of us blessed with warm memories of family, the mere mention of the word "home" conjures sentimental images. The sights, sounds and smells are all familiar; every sense thrills to the sweetness of home. Weary travelers feel drawn to it as to a cherished quilt, longing to be wrapped once more in the security of unconditional love and acceptance. Home allows us to relax our shoulders, be ourselves and leave our burdens at the door. Most of us can relate to the pleasure of being in our own homes, but how blessed we are when we can be made to feel at home when we are away from home!

Moving away from family and friends so my husband, Joe, could begin law school was not a welcome change for me, but I prayed during the months before our move that God would prepare places for both of us in our new city. The one hope we clung to was that we would have a church family waiting for us there. Our first Sunday in our new city, a young couple invited us to join them for lunch after the morning worship service. They mentioned that with classes starting at the university the next week, they had prepared for any visitors the new school year might bring.

Although this couple probably forgot the casual invitation that Joe and I couldn't even accept that day, I will never forget it. To me, it was more than an invitation to share a meal. It was a powerful reminder that no matter where we go, if God's people gather there, His arms will be opened to us. And wherever the Lord's church

meets, we can know we have a home. That lesson has been reit-
erated to us through the years as we have moved several times.
Many times we have anxiously entered a new community feeling
isolated and lonely, only to be welcomed into a church family with
open arms. In fact, many of our closest friendships have developed
as the result of Christians who have graciously and cheerfully
shared their homes with us.

The Importance of Hospitality

As God's children, we demonstrate our obedience to Him when
we practice hospitality. Romans 12:10-13 commands us to give to
one another in this way as part of being "devoted to one another
in brotherly love." To practice hospitality, we must make it a priority. It must be a charge we take seriously and something we continually strive to do. The importance of hospitality in God's eyes is
revealed in other passages, as well. In the qualifications listed for
elders, 1 Timothy 3:2 and Titus 1:8 say the overseer is to be hospitable. Scripture commands us to show hospitality to other
Christians, strangers and souls in need.

God desires that we practice hospitality as a church body because we will grow in our love for each other as a result. The early church reaped the benefits of fellowship. Acts 2:41-47 gives
the exciting details of the establishment of the Lord's church.
Reading this passage, you can sense the enthusiasm of the early
Christians and their sincere desire to be with one another. Verses
42 and 43 read,

> And they were continually devoting themselves to the
> apostles' teaching and to fellowship, to the breaking of
> bread and to prayer. And everyone kept feeling a sense
> of awe; and many wonders and signs were taking place
> through the apostles.

The faith of the early church was strengthened because the
Christians spent so much time together. The times of fellowship,
Bible study and prayer that they shared together were uplifting
and fruitful. As verses 46 and 47 attest, their commitment to hospitality helped the kingdom grow:

> And day by day continuing with one mind in the temple,

and breaking bread from house to house, they were taking their meals together with gladness and sincerity of heart, praising God, and having favor with all the people. And the Lord was adding to their number day by day those who were being saved.

Practicing hospitality gives us an opportunity to minister to souls in need. Jesus advised in Luke 14:12-14 not to be hospitable only to people who can reciprocate. Instead, He urges us to invite the destitute and downtrodden who have no means to repay our kindness. Opening our hearts and homes to people in need gives them an opportunity to experience the love of God and may help plant a seed in someone who needs the Lord.

It is easier to serve graciously and eagerly when we see people through God's eyes. We are all His beloved children. "Do not neglect to show hospitality to strangers, for by this some have entertained angels without knowing it," Hebrews 13:2 reminds us. This passage refers to Abraham and Sarah, who entertained angels in Genesis 18. We should be no less excited to serve other mortals today because all men and women are spiritual beings created by God. Furthermore, when we are hospitable to the people we meet, we are really ministering to Christ. What an honor! As Jesus told His followers in Matthew 25:40, "Truly I say to you, to the extent that you did it to one of these brothers of Mine, even the least of them, you did it to Me."

Opening Our Hearts Is the Key

No matter what kind of dwellings we live in, we can extend friendship and hospitality. Although a certain intimacy is achieved by entertaining in the home, opportunities abound for hospitality outside the home. Being hospitable might mean visiting a shut-in, calling someone who is facing a personal struggle, or taking a special interest in visitors at church. A trip to a tea room might provide a perfect opportunity to bond with a new sister in Christ, or an afternoon play date at the zoo might provide fun and fellowship for young mothers.

My friend Lisa, whose kitchen was being remodeled, once planned a special picnic that is still a cherished memory. Vonda, Kelly and

I arrived at a park to find a beautifully set table, complete with fresh flowers and party favors. Under a canopy of trees we sat in the fresh spring air nibbling layered pea salad, strawberry soup, egg salad croissants and other dainty treats. The picnic was held on the grounds of a historic home, so after a leisurely lunch we toured the house together. The whole afternoon was a lovely experience for our merry group, and even the rain shower that sent us running to the car with picnic supplies couldn't spoil our fun.

Lisa was graciously able to extend her hand in friendship because she understood that hospitality is not so much about opening your home as it is about opening your heart. In fact, the best hostess is simply a friend – someone who is willing to share her life and time. With empathy and understanding, she is always willing to listen and quick to offer encouragement. Proverbs 27:9 says, "Oil and perfume make the heart glad, So a man's counsel is sweet to his friend." Friends we know we can count on in times of joy, crisis or pain are the ones who touch us the most. When we seek to practice hospitality as Christians, we must realize that hospitality at its core is less about meeting people's physical needs and more about meeting their spiritual and emotional needs.

Serving with Graciousness

Our attitude when we practice hospitality is of utmost importance to our Lord. First Peter 4:9 urges, "Be hospitable to one another without complaint." This is an important point to put into practice if we are to serve effectively. We must cultivate a good attitude long before guests arrive.

Perfectionism can be a nasty culprit here. Worrying about presenting a picture of domestic perfection is a heavy load to bear, and we, our families and our guests will suffer from this attitude. If we are anxious and short-tempered before company arrives, we create a stressful environment for our loved ones and rob ourselves of the joy of hospitality. If we feel overwhelmed, panicked or distracted with our preparations for company, how can we expect to change our disposition when the doorbell rings and welcome guests into a calm, relaxed and inviting home?

Graciousness plays an important part in being a good hostess. Our attitude can make such a difference in how we and our guests experience our time together. We rob ourselves of joy when we focus on the difficulties of serving demanding or disagreeable guests. We forget that our reward is in heaven when we lament hard work that goes unappreciated. "Better is a dry morsel and quietness with it Than a house full of feasting with strife," Proverbs 17:1 acknowledges. If we commit within ourselves to practice hospitality without complaint, we will be able to serve eagerly and joyfully. As a result, our guests will feel more at home and our relationships with them will be strengthened.

A sense of humor will go a long way toward being a good hostess. I have certainly been humbled on many occasions when entertaining, but I am learning to laugh at myself and make the best of the situation. I still get teased on occasion for a cooking mistake I made early in my marriage, but how was I to know that the "sweet milk" my chicken pot pie recipe called for was not sweetened condensed milk? Years later, I still have to overcome embarrassing situations. Right before friends walked through the door to join us for Sunday lunch not too long ago, I dumped the casserole on our kitchen floor. What could we do but clean up the mess and laugh? I told our guests that was the first time I had ever followed the recipe for poppy seed chicken and wound up with fried chicken. We still managed to have a wonderful visit that afternoon, and one of our guests told us she would be happy to come over anytime for "upside-down poppy seed chicken."

For many families, the holidays provide a wonderful time to visit relatives separated by time and distance, allowing us to rekindle important friendships. These special days can also be sources of great stress and dread, however, if we lose the proper focus. Keeping a proper attitude toward hospitality will minimize the negative emotions that can surface as the holidays approach. Joe and I were thrilled the first time we were able to serve as hosts for our extended families at Thanksgiving. Together we decorated our home, planned menus and arranged activities. Throughout our holiday preparations, we tried to keep a spiritual focus on the special times ahead. As the holiday drew closer, I began praying daily for each person who would be in our home. After approaching the throne of God on behalf of our family members, I felt even closer to each one and was even more eager to see them face to face. We all joyfully worked together to prepare a simple yet tasty Thanksgiving feast, and after our meal, we gathered in the living room to pray, read scriptures, sing hymns and share what we were thankful for. Joe and I still talk about the wonderful memories we made that year.

Coming Home to God

Walking through the doors of a church building should feel like coming home for lost and wandering souls. Recall the parable of the prodigal sons, as told in Luke 15:11-32. Filled with shame after squandering his inheritance, the younger son returned to his father's house hoping for servant status. He got a very different reception, however, as verse 20 states: "But when he was still a great way off, his father saw him and had compassion, and ran and fell on his neck and kissed him" (NKJV). This repentant son's father welcomed him back with open arms and celebrated his return with great festivity. We should be as eager to welcome penitent souls into our church family. The sad fact is that when sinners seeking redemption come into our midst, if they do not feel embraced by the love of Christ, we may never have the opportunity to teach them further. Certainly we must adhere to biblical patterns of worship and church organization, but we cannot forget God's command that we show love. "By this all men will know that you are My disciples, if you have love for one another," John 13:35 says.

Most visitors to our congregations are less concerned with being right than they are about being loved. They may not check our doctrine at the door, but they will look for compassion. As Christian women, we can tremendously impact the kingdom of God by showing hospitality to these precious souls. Seeking out visitors, showing appreciation for their presence, and demonstrating a genuine interest in them are important first steps toward making them feel welcome. Beyond this, seeking opportunities to interact with them one-on-one outside the church building can make them feel more at ease in our congregation. A shared meal, a well-timed phone call or a follow-up visit might plant seeds for future study. It is not always easy to reach out to new people, but our efforts are vital to the growth of the church.

Anticipating and preparing ahead for visitors will make it easier to respond immediately when the need arises. Many times we set ourselves up to miss opportunities to practice hospitality. If we have piles of dirty laundry all over the floor and no food in the refrigerator, we will probably not consider extending a lunch invitation to visitors to our Sunday morning worship service. Certainly we cannot always be ready to entertain at a moment's notice, but being perpetually unprepared may reveal something about our intentions.

Practicing hospitality to visitors or new members needs to be a priority. Our hectic schedules may make it difficult to make immediate plans, but it is important that we make time to get to know new souls. When a Sunday morning visitor comes to your congregation, you might find yourself unprepared for company the first Sunday, out of town the second, committed to lunch plans with another family the third, and hosting out-of-town relatives the fourth. How quickly a month can pass before it becomes convenient to reach out to a visitor who may feel unwelcome and discouraged by that time. Even the smallest gesture, such as sharing a meal at a restaurant or inviting visitors to join a previously scheduled activity, can begin forming the bonds of fellowship.

For What It's Worth

At its core, hospitality is less about meeting the physical needs of people and more about meeting their spiritual and emotional needs. Like Lydia, we can impact the kingdom of God by extending our hands in friendship and hospitality. Scripture encourages us to reach out to fellow Christians, strangers and souls in need. We are to serve with graciousness, humility and cheerfulness, always seeking opportunities to minister to our guests. If we take seriously God's command to practice hospitality, we will grow in the grace of giving, minister to lost souls, encourage the saints, and develop friendships that will sustain us throughout life.

Give an Answer

1. Read the account of Lydia's conversion in Acts 16:11-40. Why was her invitation to Paul and Silas significant?
2. Of what importance was fellowship to the growth of the early church (Acts 2:41-47)?
3. What can we learn about hospitality from Luke 14:12-14?

4. Relate Proverbs 27:9 to being a good hostess.
5. Why are Proverbs 17:1 and 1 Peter 4:9 important to keep in mind?
6. Read Luke 15:11-32. To what lengths did this father go to welcome his prodigal son home?

Give It Some Thought

1. Why do we sometimes feel intimidated to invite people into our homes? How can we overcome our insecurities?
2. Share a time when you were blessed by the hospitality of a Christian sister. What made your time together memorable?
3. What role does having a good attitude play in being a good hostess?
4. Why is it important to prepare for opportunities to show hospitality?
5. Name some ways we can make church visitors feel welcome.

Give It a Try

1. Invite neighbors to your home for a brunch, dessert party or cookout.
2. Plan an afternoon tea for a shut-in. Fill a basket with hot tea, dainty sandwiches and fresh flowers to share during a lovely bedside visit.
3. Anticipate the arrival of visitors to your worship service by preparing extra food for your Sunday lunch. If you don't have any visitors, extend an invitation to someone in the congregation you don't know well.

CHAPTER 5

PLEASED
TO SERVE

"Therefore, since we receive a kingdom which cannot be shaken, let us show gratitude, by which we may offer to God an acceptable service with reverence and awe" (Hebrews 12:28).

Seeking anonymity, she slipped past the group of women in the marketplace with her head down. Although she avoided their eyes, she still felt penetrated by their gaze. She knew they were judging her. Hard living had aged her once lovely features, and she carried the weight of her sins on drooping shoulders. She was weary of the life she had created, embarrassed that her mistakes were fodder for gossip in the streets. Her face flushed knowing that a frenzy of stinging whispers would erupt to condemn her even before she was out of earshot.

She caught a sliver of the ladies' conversation as she passed. "Yes, I have heard His teachings," she heard one of them say. "He is at Simon's house now." She knew they were talking about Jesus. News of the Prophet had reached the city even before He came. Throughout the region He had healed diseases, given sight to the blind, made the lame to walk, and even raised the dead. Always careful to stay in the shadows of the crowd, she had listened to Him preach. Even from a distance she could tell that He was different from the other religious men of her day.

"If only I could get close to Him," she thought. "Perhaps He would have mercy on me, an unworthy sinner. My sins are so great, though. He might feel dirtied by my uncleanness. Would He take pity on me, or would He be repulsed and turn me away?"

As she continued walking, she considered the scenes she had

witnessed since Jesus had been in town. On many occasions she had seen Him welcome the sick and poor into His presence without hesitation. He had willingly healed lepers and ministered to many people the rest of the world shunned. His compassionate nature was such a contrast to the smug attitude of the other religious teachers she had known, but could He really be different?

Deep in thought, she barely noticed that she was home. Walking through her front door, her brow furrowed as she wondered if she would ever have an opportunity to talk with Jesus. Who could say how long He would be in town? She now felt eager to speak with Him, but the women in the marketplace had said He was at Simon's house. A respected Pharisee, Simon would not want to be seen with a sinner like her. She knew he would never invite her to enter his home, but she felt desperate enough to see the Teacher to risk rejection. She knew one thing with certainty: She could not continue this way of life.

Determined now to see Jesus, her gaze settled on her only possession of worth, a vial of perfume. As she noticed the white alabaster bottle gleaming in the sunlight, an idea began to form. Without a second thought she clutched the perfume to her chest and dashed into the street.

Her feet took her quickly to Simon's house. Through the window she could see Jesus and the other men still talking. Her stomach fluttered and her throat tightened as she considered what might happen when she entered Simon's house uninvited, but she pushed her fears aside. She knew what she had to do. And with tears welling in her eyes, she summoned all the courage in her heart and reached out to open the door.

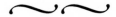

Reading about this unnamed woman in Luke 7:36-50, we know what happened next. While Jesus was a guest in the home of Simon, verses 37 and 38 tell us,

> And behold, there was a woman in the city who was a sinner; and when she learned that He was reclining at the table in the Pharisee's house, she brought an alabaster vial of perfume, and standing behind Him at His

feet, weeping, she began to wet His feet with her tears, and kept wiping them with the hair of her head, and kissing His feet, and anointing them with the perfume.

Simon, incredulous at this sight, told himself that if Jesus were really a prophet, He would know that this woman was sinful and would not let her touch Him. With a parable of two debtors who were unable to repay their debts, Jesus showed Simon that those who are forgiven more will love their master more.

The heart of this passage is verses 44-47:

> And turning toward the woman, He said to Simon, "Do you see this woman? I entered your house; you gave Me no water for My feet, but she has wet My feet with her tears, and wiped them with her hair. You gave Me no kiss; but she, since the time I came in, has not ceased to kiss My feet. You did not anoint My head with oil, but she anointed My feet with perfume. For this reason I say to you, her sins, which are many, have been forgiven, for she loved much; but he who is forgiven little, loves little."

Then before the eyes of the critical Pharisees, Jesus told the woman that her sins had been forgiven, her faith had saved her, and she could go away in peace.

What a poignant example we have in this woman of courage mingled with humility. First, think about the boldness it must have taken for her to approach Jesus in the house of Simon. She risked humiliation and rejection entering the midst of the Pharisees, yet she did it anyway. Second, consider her generosity. That alabaster bottle of perfume surely would have been one of her most costly possessions, yet she willingly gave it to Jesus. Finally, this woman could have presented her gift with great fanfare, but instead she presented it with the greatest humility. As her tears fell on Jesus' feet, she wiped them with her hair, kissed them, and anointed them with oil. What a loving act of service this was.

In the eyes of the Pharisees and her fellow citizens, this woman was a sinner, but Jesus recognized her as His child. She was willing to humble herself before the Lord and give Him her broken spirit, and in return Jesus gave her a new beginning. Because of her faith, He forgave her sins and sent her away to a new life of hope and peace. How her grateful heart must have rejoiced as she left Simon's home!

Perhaps the most interesting point of this passage is who Jesus pointed to as the example. In this room full of Pharisees, men who were considered great religious people, the person who taught the greatest spiritual lesson that day was the sinful woman crawling on the floor. Without saying a word, she spoke volumes about generosity, humility and courage. Our challenge for this chapter is to cultivate our giving as this unnamed woman did by offering ourselves in humble service.

Christians Lead Through Service

As Christian women, there is much we can do to serve in the kingdom of God, yet sometimes we may be tempted to focus on the few things Scripture does not permit us to do. As women gain equal footing with men in the workplace and in society, it can be tempting to apply our earthly concepts of leadership and equality to the church and feel disgruntled that we do not have biblical authority to assume positions of leadership or take public roles in worship. When we focus on public leadership and neglect the areas where we are commanded to serve, we fall prey to the world's ideas of greatness. As Christians, we have a higher calling. Instead of seeking lofty positions or desiring greater status, we should focus on being the kind of leaders Christ described: "But the greatest among you shall be your servant. And whoever exalts himself shall be humbled; and whoever humbles himself shall be exalted" (Matthew 23:11-12). True Christian leadership comes through service.

As Christians struggling with earthly concepts of greatness, we find ourselves in good company. Many biblical characters sought worldly recognition for their good deeds, including Ananias and Sapphira (Acts 5:1-11) and Simon the Sorcerer (8:18-24). Even Christ's apostles sought status in the kingdom. In Matthew 20:20-21, the mother of James and John asked Jesus if her sons could be seated to the left and right of Jesus in the kingdom to come; and Luke 22:24 says a dispute arose among the apostles regarding who was the greatest. Jesus' response to the apostles regarding greatness in the kingdom of God is the same for us today:

> [W]hoever wishes to become great among you shall be
> your servant, and whoever wishes to be first among you
> shall be your slave; just as the Son of Man did not come
> to be served, but to serve, and to give His life a ransom
> for many (Matthew 20:26-28).

It is through our most humble acts of service that we will truly achieve glory in the kingdom of God. I have often wondered, if at the end of our lives we could each ask God to reveal our greatest deed in His eyes, whether we would be surprised at what He would choose. I believe many of us would not even remember the act that He would choose because it probably would have been some random act of service that had been carried out with humility and quickly forgotten.

Our acts of service may not bring much in the way of worldly praise or prestige in this life, but they will not be forgotten by our Lord. Through service, we have tremendous capacity to demonstrate leadership in the church. When we possess humility and compassion, our good deeds can help lead people to Christ and draw them into closer communion with their church family. Truly, in God's eyes, to serve is to lead.

The Nitty-Gritty of Giving

Every congregation is blessed to have members who work behind the scenes to keep worship services running smoothly. Without seeking praise or prestige, these individuals quietly organize classrooms, fill communion cups, count the collection, tidy church pews, arrange flowers, fix leaking pipes, maintain the grounds and do myriad other anonymous tasks. These same people are also usually the first to volunteer to meet needs outside the church building. At a moment's notice they are willing to change a tire, take an elderly sister to the doctor, provide child care for a sick mother, offer transportation for vacation Bible school, prepare care packages for college students, clean the home of a sick friend, or load a moving truck. With meekness they minister to the needy, from time to time filling gas tanks, stocking pantries or settling unpaid debts. Preferring to do their good deeds in the shadows, these servants go about their daily lives quietly giving through acts of service.

Our focus for this chapter is on service, meaning the often difficult, thankless, anonymous tasks that require us to humble ourselves to do them. These deeds are usually only noticed when they are not done. By doing tasks which may be undesirable or unpopular, we obey and glorify God. Hebrews 12:28-29 urges,

> Therefore, since we receive a kingdom which cannot be shaken, let us show gratitude, by which we may offer to God an acceptable service with reverence and awe; for our God is a consuming fire.

Through our service, we demonstrate thankfulness for our salvation. No price should be too great for us to pay in this life when we consider the price our Lord paid for our hope of eternal life.

As Galatians 5:13-14 points out, we show our love for the people around us when we minister to them: "[T]hrough love serve one another. For the whole Law is fulfilled in one word, in the statement, 'You shall love your neighbor as yourself.' " Consider a mother's love for her child. Her concern for the health, comfort and safety of her child will lead her to do many things that would have sounded unpleasant to her before she met and fell in love with her baby. Consider this list of tasks:

- change dirty diapers
- wipe runny noses
- scrub crayon marks off walls
- spend sleepless nights fighting fevers
- provide discipline
- offer taxi services
- help with school reports first mentioned the day before they are due
- learn the subtleties of countless sports and hobbies
- sacrifice desires for new clothing or furniture

Who would rush to apply for a job with this description? Few of us would say we enjoy the tasks listed above, yet without complaint a mother will do these and more – all in the name of love. When we truly love other people as God loves us, serving them is not difficult. Our love for them will open our eyes to their needs and help propel us toward acts of kindness on their behalf.

Giving through serving often requires that we humble ourselves.

As Jesus said in John 12:24, "Truly, truly, I say to you, unless a grain of wheat falls into the earth and dies, it remains by itself alone; but if it dies, it bears much fruit." In order to reach our full potential in the kingdom, we must empty ourselves of selfishness, vanity and pride. If we are willing to die to ourselves and give our lives to God, we can do great things for the kingdom. Heaven will be ours if we are willing to use our lives in service to our Lord, as Jesus promised in verses 25-26:

> He who loves his life loses it; and he who hates his life in this world shall keep it to life eternal. If anyone serves Me, let him follow Me; and where I am, there shall My servant also be; if anyone serves Me, the Father will honor him.

Although acts of service done with compassion and humility often will not bring earthly glory, our Father will notice and reward our faithfulness.

Servants of Christ

King David, the most powerful man of his time, recognized his need for submission to God. He wrote in Psalm 116:16-17,

> O Lord, surely I am Thy servant,
> I am Thy servant, the son of Thy handmaid,
> Thou hast loosed my bonds.
> To Thee I shall offer a sacrifice of thanksgiving,
> And call upon the name of the Lord.

If this God-ordained world leader could view himself as a servant, then we too should be able to humble ourselves to serve God with meekness and modesty.

As we consider the humility our relationship with God requires, it is profitable to take a look at scriptures written about how slaves were to carry out their service. As Christians, we are servants of Christ and He is our Master. Ephesians 6:5-8 says,

> Slaves, be obedient to those who are your masters according to the flesh, with fear and trembling, in the sincerity of your heart, as to Christ; not by way of eyeservice, as men-pleasers, but as slaves of Christ, doing the

will of God from the heart. With good will render service, as to the Lord, and not to men, knowing that whatever good thing each one does, this he will receive back
from the Lord, whether slave or free.

As slaves of righteousness, it is our duty and great honor to give
ourselves in acts of service for God's glory. Our Master will be
most pleased when we do.

Our attitude in service is of utmost importance. It is not just our
acts of service, but also the way we serve, that will please God. We
are to be humble, compassionate, sincere, steadfast and spiritually minded. Colossians 3:22 instructs, "Slaves, in all things obey
those who are your masters on earth, not with external service, as
those who merely please men, but with sincerity of heart, fear-
ing the Lord." We must continually strive to keep our focus on God
to avoid losing the proper attitude.

Our service to God is a matter of eternal consequence. In
Matthew 24:45-51, Christ talked about His second coming and the
duty we have to work until His return. Our active service will please
Him. If we forget our purpose on earth, however, we can become
lax in our service to God. In the end, we will regret our inaction.
As Christians, we must continually seek opportunities to minister
to the people around us. Doing so earnestly and compassionately will please our Master.

For What It's Worth

In the story of the unnamed woman of Luke 7:36-50, we see a
poignant example of humility and courage intertwined. In the home
of Simon the Pharisee, she kissed Jesus' feet, washed them with
her tears, anointed them with oil, and dried them with her hair.
Her compassionate act of service touched Jesus and demonstrated her penitent heart. When we are able to empty ourselves of vanity, pride and selfishness, we too will be able to give ourselves to
God in acts of service. Although these tasks are often difficult,
thankless and anonymous, our Father in heaven will notice and reward our good deeds. If we recognize ourselves as slaves of Christ,
we can meekly serve Him with joy and earnestness. Doing so, we
will cultivate the grace of giving and fulfill Christ's definition of
leadership through servanthood.

Give an Answer

1. Compare the unnamed woman's service to the Pharisee's actions (Luke 3:36-50). How did Jesus respond to the woman's act of service?
2. According to John 12:24, what must we be willing to do in order to bear fruit in the kingdom of God?
3. How does Galatians 5:13-14 translate into service?
4. Why does knowing the author of Psalm 116:16-17 make the passage more significant?
5. How does Colossians 3:22-24 apply to us, and what can we learn from this passage?
6. Relate Matthew 24:45-51 to Christians today.

Give It Some Thought

1. Describe "acts of service," as discussed in this chapter. Why might examples of what one considers an act of service be different from sister to sister?
2. What steps can we take to empty ourselves of vanity, pride and selfishness to prepare ourselves for service to God?
3. How does the biblical example of leadership differ from that of the world?
4. Share a time when you were touched by a good deed. Why was this act of service meaningful?
5. What role does our love for people play in our willingness to find opportunities to serve them?

Give It a Try

1. Find out who in your congregation is responsible for a seldom recognized task, and take a moment to encourage that person by voicing your appreciation or writing a note of thanks.
2. Sing a hymn such as "O to Be Like Thee," "O Master, Let Me Walk with Thee," "Purer in Heart, O God" or "More Holiness Give Me." Reflect on ways you can humble yourself for service.
3. Pick a name out of the church directory at random, and do an anonymous act of kindness for that person.

CHAPTER 6

LAY DOWN YOUR TREASURES

"Instruct them to do good, to be rich in good works, to be generous and ready to share, storing up for themselves the treasure of a good foundation for the future, so that they may take hold of that which is life indeed" (1 Timothy 6:18-19).

Hannah hummed softly as she rubbed her swollen belly, daydreaming about the precious child growing within her womb. She had waited so long to have a baby, but her anticipation to see and touch this child made these last days seem the longest. She could hardly wait to hold her infant for the first time – to caress its soft skin, hear its first gurgles and feel those tiny fingers curl around hers.

Hannah loved her role as Elkanah's wife, but her greatest desire had always been to be a mother. The years of waiting to conceive had been trying, made almost unbearable at times by the cruel taunting of Elkanah's other wife. Hannah had tried to mask her feelings before Peninnah, but to no avail. Try as she might to steel herself against the evil things her rival would say, too often bitter tears would betray her emotions. In her grief, Hannah would not be able to eat or sleep for days.

Elkanah was a loving and supportive husband, and his tender words soothed Hannah; but her only real solace came from the Lord. A woman of prayer, Hannah approached the throne of God regularly to give her cares to the Lord and to plead for a child. The last time she accompanied Elkanah to Shiloh, Hannah poured out her heart to the Lord in the temple. She promised the Lord then that if He would give her a son, she would consecrate him to the Lord's service all the days of his life.

Determined to fulfill her vow, already Hannah sang hymns, quoted Scripture and prayed aloud so the child in her womb would come to know the supremacy of the Lord even before birth. She was eager to share the exciting stories of God's providential care for her people, and she planned to instill an attitude of reverence toward the family's visits to the temple.

A sudden kick startled Hannah and brought forth a giggle. "My, but you are active today, aren't you, little one?"

"Perhaps he is ready to make his way into the world," Hannah thought. "He." She caught herself, and smiled. "My son will be called Samuel because I asked for Him from the Lord. Great is the Lord God of Israel. Great He is indeed."

The hill country of Ephraim sets the stage for our story, found in the first two chapters of 1 Samuel. There Elkanah lived with his two wives, Hannah and Peninnah. Peninnah had children, but Hannah, the favored wife, was barren. Each year Elkanah and his family would journey to Shiloh to worship and offer sacrifices in the temple. On the day of sacrifice, Elkanah would give Hannah double portions because he loved her. These trips were still difficult for Hannah because of Peninnah's harassment. Elkanah tried to comfort her but could not fully comprehend her pain.

Hannah found solace in prayer to God at the temple. She vowed to the Lord that if He would give her a son, she would consecrate him to the Lord. Priest Eli observed her fervent prayer and thought she was drunk. "No, my lord, I am a woman oppressed in spirit; I have drunk neither wine nor strong drink, but I have poured out my soul before the Lord," she revealed in 1 Samuel 1:15-16. "Do not consider your maidservant as a worthless woman; for I have spoken until now out of my great concern and provocation." Eli sent Hannah away in peace, hopeful that God would grant her petition for a son.

The depth of Hannah's trust in God, which is revealed in verse 18, foreshadows her depth of commitment demonstrated later in the story. After her prayer to God, Hannah went away with a spirit of contentment. She was able to leave her worries with the Lord and join her family to eat and worship. Her trust was rewarded, and she gave birth to Samuel.

Hannah did not forget the promise she made to the Lord. When the time came for Elkanah and his household to make their yearly trip to the temple, Hannah stayed behind.

> But Hannah did not go up, for she said to her husband, "I will not go up until the child is weaned; then I will bring him, that he may appear before the Lord and stay there forever" (1:22).

After Samuel was weaned, she demonstrated her faithfulness to the vow she made before God. Hannah took Samuel to the house of the Lord and delivered him to Eli. How difficult it must have been for Hannah to make that trip, knowing that she would part with her son. Her heart must have ached for her baby, yet it must also have swelled with pride knowing that her son would be used in service to the Lord.

One of the most remarkable aspects of this story is the beautiful prayer Hannah prayed after consecrating her son for service to the Lord. In 1 Samuel 2:1-10, Hannah again poured out her heart to God, this time in praise and thankfulness. Her prayer began,

> My heart exults in the Lord;
> My horn is exalted in the Lord,
> My mouth speaks boldly against my enemies,
> Because I rejoice in Thy salvation.
> There is no one holy like the Lord,
> Indeed, there is no one besides Thee,
> Nor is there any rock like our God (vv. 1-2).

On and on she prayed in praise and adoration of God. Her prayer focused not on herself and her loss, but on the supremacy and sovereignty of God.

Hannah was rewarded for her faithfulness. Each year she would visit Samuel in the temple and deliver a new robe she had made for him. How it must have pleased her to see him becoming a man of God. The Lord remembered Hannah's sacrifice and blessed her with three more sons and two daughters.

As a mother, it is difficult to imagine how Hannah could give up her son. After waiting so long to have a child, Samuel must have filled Hannah's heart with pride. How she must have savored every fleeting moment of his infancy and cherished every memory of their time together. How difficult it must have been to part with him, knowing she would see him only once a year. Her thoughts must have gone to him often over the years, wondering what he was learning and how he might be serving in the temple.

The Lord blessed Hannah throughout her life because of her faithfulness. Because she asked Him for a child and then trusted Him to provide, He gave her a son. When she consecrated Samuel to God with joyfulness, the Lord watched over the young boy and communicated with him in the temple. During their yearly visits to Shiloh, Hannah was able to continue a relationship with Samuel and see him becoming a man of God. Priest Eli saw the faithfulness of Samuel's parents and each year asked the Lord to bless Elkanah and Hannah with more children. God did remember Hannah with five more children.

Hannah's faithfulness to her promise and her sacrificial attitude serve as an example for us today. A woman in Hannah's situation could have fulfilled her promise to the Lord with bitterness or regret, but Scripture indicates that Hannah was honored to dedicate Samuel to the Lord's service. Although we might expect the time she gave Samuel back to God to have been the darkest point of her life, Hannah prayed a beautiful prayer of thanksgiving after delivering Samuel to the temple. No doubt, Samuel must have been his mother's joy and purpose, yet she loved the Lord even more than her heart's greatest treasure. As we strive to increase the worth of our giving, let us follow Hannah's example in our willingness to sacrifice our treasures for the Lord.

Our Treasure Is in Heaven

It is God's will that we learn to sacrifice our treasures. Our treasures are the blessings we hold most dear. These will differ from person to person. For one, career advancement, professional reputation or possessions might be important. For another, physical appearance, educational achievement or athletic prowess might be a major concern. Whatever our earthly treasures might be, we must realize their temporal nature. Our only real treasures will be found in heaven. First Peter 2:5 reminds us that "you also, as living stones, are being built up as a spiritual house for a holy priesthood, to offer up spiritual sacrifices acceptable to God through Jesus Christ." What an honor it is to consider that we are being prepared to offer sacrifices to God as a holy priesthood. Keeping this in mind will help us give eagerly, joyfully and reverently.

We please God when we use our blessings to His glory. Anyone can give away what she does not want, but truly sacrificing is more difficult. Giving up your greatest treasure takes commitment. We must develop attitudes of selflessness in order to share our treasures. Jesus commanded us in Matthew 6:19-21,

> Do not lay up for yourselves treasures upon earth, where moth and rust destroy, and where thieves break in and steal. But lay up for yourselves treasures in heaven, where neither moth nor rust destroys, and where thieves do not break in or steal; for where your treasure is, there will your heart be also.

When we give sacrificially, we demonstrate trust in God and acknowledge that the temporal blessings of this world come from Him. The blessings of this life are fleeting, but God's promises are eternal. Realizing that our greatest treasures will be found in heaven allows us to let go of our earthly treasures and give them back to the One who gave them to us.

Heaven's Treasure Seekers

Failing to see beyond this life makes it difficult even to conceive of giving sacrificially. Consider the rich young ruler of Matthew 19. His countenance fell when Jesus told him in verse 21, "If you wish to be complete, go and sell your possessions and give to the poor, and you shall have treasure in heaven; and come, follow Me." He found security and happiness in his earthly possessions and missed Jesus' promise of treasure in heaven. Moses, on the other hand, was willing to sacrifice status and riches because he was able to look beyond his immediate desires. Hebrews 11:24-26 says,

> By faith Moses, when he had grown up, refused to be called the son of Pharaoh's daughter; choosing rather to endure ill-treatment with the people of God, than to

enjoy the passing pleasures of sin; considering the reproach of Christ greater riches than the treasures of Egypt; for he was looking to the reward.

Keeping our eyes fixed on the world to come will help us to follow the examples of Moses and Hannah, who were willing to pay any price to serve God.

People today who have been touched by the love of Jesus are willing to share their treasures, as well. Preachers sacrifice job security and financial gain in order to share the gospel. Missionaries leave the comforts of home and family to spread the gospel to people in distant lands. Elders' and deacons' families give their love and commitment to the local church, and Bible school teachers share their wisdom and time to help their pupils grow spiritually. As Christians, we all can share our treasures to benefit the kingdom of God. As our devotion to the Lord grows, we will find more and more opportunities to sacrifice our time, talents and resources for God's glory.

The Heart Won't Lie

Maintaining a sacrificial attitude is not easy. Although we may say that God is most dear to us, our hearts often tell a different story. Many of us hope that we would stand strong if faced with religious persecution on a grand scale, yet we may falter with smaller tests of our faithfulness. Keeping our Christian walk comfortable can render us complacent and unmotivated to sacrifice. First Timothy 6:17-19 is aimed at people who feel financially secure, but could also apply to anyone who has found false security in this life. This passage reminds us not to fix our hopes on the uncertainty of riches but on God. Verses 18-19 urge,

> Instruct them to do good, to be rich in good works, to
> be generous and ready to share, storing up for them-
> selves the treasure of a good foundation for the future,
> so that they may take hold of that which is life indeed.

We must not let earthly riches or easy religion make us forget our dependence on God and our need to give sacrificially to Him.

Our relationship with God should be our hearts' greatest treasure, but worldly possessions or ideals can draw us away if we are not watchful. Losing sight of our purpose in this world endangers our willingness to sacrifice for the cause of Christ. By changing focus, we lose perspective on our lives and blessings. This allows the priorities of the world to become more important to us than giving to the Lord. Romans 12:1 urges us to keep our eyes on God in order to maintain a sacrificial spirit: "[P]resent your bodies a living and holy sacrifice, acceptable to God, which is your spiritual service of worship." When we keep our spirits focused on the Lord, our hearts and minds will be continually refreshed by Him, and we will find new opportunities every day to sacrifice for His glory.

A Sacrifice of Thanks

King David knew that his willingness to give was a direct reflection of his thankfulness for God's care and protection. Brimming with gratitude, his psalms often express a desire to sacrifice to the Lord. Psalm 54:6 says, "Willingly I will sacrifice to Thee; I will give thanks to Thy name, O Lord, for it is good." Psalm 116:17 says, "To Thee I shall offer a sacrifice of thanksgiving, And call upon the name of the Lord." We studied previously how the king refused to make an offering to the Lord which cost him nothing (2 Samuel 24:10-25). He understood that a sacrifice without cost does not really express gratitude, and he lived his life always ready to give the Lord his treasures.

We are to be thankful for the gifts God gives us. This thankfulness is best expressed by our using these blessings to His glory. Ephesians 5:1-2 urges, "Therefore be imitators of God, as beloved children; and walk in love, just as Christ also loved you, and gave Himself up for us, an offering and a sacrifice to God as a fragrant aroma." Christ gave His life for us as the ultimate sacrifice for our sins. We owe Him no less than to use our lives and all the blessings at our disposal to His glory.

God does not require us to discard our blessings, but we should use them in a way that honors and pleases Him. God does not ask us to give away our homes, for example, but He does ask us to use them to practice hospitality. We displease God when we try to bury our treasures or hoard them for our own use. Blessings are meant to be shared. Let us strive to give our hearts' greatest treasures to the Lord so that we may present ourselves as living sacrifices for the good of the kingdom.

God Will Reward Our Sacrifice

Perhaps no Bible character exemplifies a spirit of sacrifice more than Paul. After his conversion, he endured many trials to further the cause of Christ. Throughout beatings, shipwrecks and imprisonments, he counted his suffering joy and found privilege in his service to the Lord. He encouraged his brethren to share his eagerness for sacrifice:

> But we have this treasure in earthen vessels, that the surpassing greatness of the power may be of God and not from ourselves; we are afflicted in every way, but not crushed; perplexed, but not despairing; persecuted, but not forsaken; struck down, but not destroyed; always carrying about in the body the dying of Jesus, that the life of Jesus also may be manifested in our body (2 Corinthians 4:7-10).

Paul found great purpose in his work for the Lord because he knew that he could never give the Lord more than the Lord had already given him. His thankfulness for his salvation made him eager to give all his resources to the Lord.

We can never surpass God's giving, no matter how much we are willing to sacrifice. God has already blessed us beyond what we could ever ask or deserve, and He is always eager to give us more. When we serve God through sharing our treasures, God is pleased and will reward our faithfulness. Jesus promised the apostles in Mark 10:29-30 that their sacrifices for His name would not go unheeded by God. The Lord assured His followers that sacrifices made for the sake of the gospel would be restored a hundred times in the present age, to be followed in the age to come by eternal life.

When we give sacrificially and with the right attitude, knowing that we are pleasing God and helping others is blessing enough. However, God's promises to provide for us and to prepare a place in heaven for us make the rewards of giving that much sweeter.

For What It's Worth

As much as Hannah loved her son, she loved the Lord more. She consecrated Samuel to the Lord's service and was rewarded for her faithfulness. God does not ask us to discard our treasures, but He expects us to use them to His glory. True sacrifice is only possible when we realize that our real treasures are being laid up in heaven. Keeping our focus on the Lord will keep us from slipping into complacency or becoming unwilling to sacrifice in our Christian walk. When we give sacrificially, we demonstrate trust in God and acknowledge that the temporal blessings of this world come from Him. Our thankfulness is best expressed by our willingness to share our blessings. When we cultivate the grace of giving through our willingness to sacrifice our hearts' treasures for His good, we will please our Father and the joys of heaven will be ours.

Give an Answer

1. Read Hannah's prayer of thanksgiving in 1 Samuel 2:1-10. What can we learn from Hannah's attitude?
2. What do Jesus' words in Matthew 6:19-21 tell us about where our focus should be?
3. According to Romans 12:1-2, what does God desire of us?
4. Who are we imitating when we give sacrificially, according to Ephesians 5:1-2?
5. How will we be compensated by the Father for sacrifices made in His name, according to Mark 10:29-30?
6. In this chapter, we have looked to Hannah, Moses, David and Paul as biblical examples of sacrifice. Can you cite others?

Give It Some Thought

1. What obstacles keep us from giving sacrificially?
2. Which resources do you find the most difficult to give?
3. Consider a special or unexpected gift that you received from a loved one. How did it make you feel? What made it special?
4. How would you describe the joy of sacrifice?
5. Discuss the sacrifices Jesus made for us when He left heaven

to become our Savior. How should this motivate us to give more?

Give It a Try

1. Write a prayer of thanksgiving in the style of Hannah's prayer, as recorded in 1 Samuel 2:1-10.
2. Rather than merely giving discarded items to your congregation's clothing center, contribute a new garment of the quality you would choose for yourself.
3. As a family project or on an individual basis, list your blessings and look for ways to use them to the glory of God.

CHAPTER 7

TIME TO GIVE

"There is an appointed time for everything. And there is a time for every event under heaven" (Ecclesiastes 3:1).

Water spattered over the mouth of her water jug as Martha hurried down the path. The good news she carried made the road seem longer than usual. At last, she saw the house she shared with her sister and brother rise in the distance. "Mary! ... Mary!" Martha called to her sister between gasps while still out of hearing range. Flushed and out of breath from rushing home, she could not speak again as she drew closer. Excitement propelled her quickly to the door, and she burst into the house.

Startled by her sister's hasty entrance, Mary dropped a bowl. The dish shattered, sending shards of jagged, broken pottery shooting across the floor. "Martha," an exasperated Mary began to scold, but she stopped abruptly when she saw Martha's face. "What is it?" Mary asked, rushing to her sister's side. She could read the excitement on Martha's face and feared that something could be wrong. "What has happened?" an alarmed Mary asked expectantly, taking Martha's hands.

After a few anxious moments that spanned an eternity, Martha caught her breath and announced: "Jesus is coming! Jesus is coming!" Mary's worry turned to joy, and she squealed with delight.

"He will be here soon," Martha continued earnestly. "We have much to do to prepare for His arrival." With this statement, her countenance changed. Already, her eagerness to see Jesus was giving way to anxiety at having company on such short notice. She pursed her lips as she considered what she needed to do first. And with her mind swimming with a litany of tasks to be done, Martha darted out the door again.

"There is much to do indeed," Mary agreed, but Martha was already gone. Mary stared for a moment at the spot where Martha had stood just seconds before, then reached for the broom and began sweeping up the pieces of pottery that littered the floor. "Jesus is coming," she thought to herself. She smiled happily as her anticipation of His visit grew. "What a special day this is! What a privilege it will be for Martha and me to sit at His feet and hear His godly message. We will be so much richer for our time spent with Him. What spiritual lessons will we learn from Him today, I wonder?"

Putting the broom aside, Mary got to work on the more pressing tasks at hand. Jesus could arrive any minute, and she wanted to be prepared to make the most of their visit with Him. Mary had so many questions for the Teacher; she hoped she would have enough time to organize her thoughts before His arrival. As she reflected on the Scriptures, her mind drifted momentarily to Martha. "Where is she?" Mary thought. "We have so much to do." Mary hoped she was bringing to mind their past religious discussions and the theological debates they had overheard in the temple. No doubt, Jesus would be able to feed their spirits with His words of wisdom. Kneeling to pray for their visit with Jesus, she hardly noticed Martha breeze through the room.

After several minutes, a knock at the door brought Mary swiftly to her feet. "Martha, Martha!" she cried. "Jesus is here! Jesus is here!"

Luke 10:38-42 is where our story unfolds. Verse 38 tells us about Jesus' arrival in Bethany: "Now as they were traveling along, He entered a certain village; and a woman named Martha welcomed Him into her home." Martha's sister, Mary, sat at Jesus' feet listening to Him speak, but verse 40 tells us that Martha was "distracted with all her preparations." She urged Jesus to scold Mary for leaving her to do all the serving alone, but Jesus rebuked Martha instead:

> Martha, Martha, you are worried and bothered about
> so many things; but only a few things are necessary, re-

ally only one, for Mary has chosen the good part, which
shall not be taken away from her (vv. 41-42).

Luke's account of Jesus' visit with Mary and Martha is not one
of the more beloved Bible stories among women with whom I have
talked. This story strikes a chord with many of us because we can
look at Martha's encounter with the Lord and see ourselves in her
shoes. We feel sympathy for her because we often find ourselves
busy with chores, just as she was. We might even feel like defending
Martha. After all, hospitality is important, isn't it? And didn't someone have to do the work that day if they were to eat? It is true that
hospitality is important; Scripture commands it, and other women
of the Bible are commended for their graciousness in extending it.
And certainly, practicing hospitality requires work. So why did Jesus
praise Mary and reprimand Martha?

Martha's key problem was in her attitude. She probably was
eager to welcome Jesus into her home when she extended the invitation, but she let her anxiety at having company skew her perspective. Scripture describes her as "distracted" in verse 40 and
"worried and bothered" in verse 41. She did not carry out her duties in a way that pleased God or made Jesus feel welcome. Still oc-
cupied when He arrived, Martha grew more agitated as she did
the chores alone while Mary sat at Jesus' feet.

Can't you picture the scene as Martha worked? I imagine she
passed by Jesus and Mary several times before speaking, each
time shooting angry looks in her sister's direction or perhaps even
sighing audibly as her impatience grew. It is interesting to note
that Martha's anxiety was evident to Jesus before she voiced her
grievance, but He did not rebuke her until she urged Him to scold
Mary. In a huff, she complained in verse 40, "Lord, do You not care
that my sister has left me to do all the serving alone? Then tell her
to help me." Because of her anxiety over earthly concerns, Martha
lost an opportunity to commune with the Lord.

Now we turn our attention to the woman who sat at Jesus' feet.
Jesus did not scold her. In fact, He praised Mary for her wise use
of time. If you think about it, how could she have better used her
time to make Jesus feel more welcome? And what else could she
have done that day that would have nourished her soul more? Mary
understood that nothing could be more important than sitting at

the feet of the Son of God and listening to His words. She was praised because she was willing to pause from the mundane tasks of her day to experience God. She took time to sit at His feet and bask in His presence. "Mary has chosen the good part," Jesus told Martha in verse 42. Her attitude and priorities pleased God.

If we had been in Bethany that day, would we have joined Mary at Jesus' feet or would we have been too busy with other chores? Certainly, we hope that if Jesus came to our homes today, we would be eager to share our time with Him. Sadly, though, we forfeit opportunities to commune with God every day because of worldly concerns. Our time is precious; we must cultivate the grace of giving through learning to give our time to God.

No Time to Waste

Psalm 39 reminds us that the nature of life is fleeting:

> Lord, make me to know my end,
> And what is the extent of my days,
> Let me know how transient I am.
> Behold, Thou hast made my days as handbreadths,
> And my lifetime as nothing in Thy sight,
> Surely every man at his best is a mere breath.
>
> (vv. 4-5)

Most of us have been shaken from our routines with news of the death of a loved one. Whether it follows a lengthy illness or comes abruptly, the death of a friend often manages to catch us off guard. We are reminded during these times that life is short. Each breath we take could be our last, and we have no guarantee that we will see another day beyond this one. Although we often rush through our days taking life for granted, absent-mindedness or indifference will not abrogate the reality that our time on earth is limited.

Truly, time is our most precious commodity. Every hour of every day, we exchange precious moments of our lives for events we deem important, such as work, sleep or play. In our culture we use many phrases to describe time. We talk about "spending" time, "having" time and "making" time. We like to think about "saving" time, but in truth, we cannot hoard this precious resource. We can only try to use our time wisely by using it to God's glory. Here is where we find the meaning of life. Proverbs 3:1-6 urges,

My son, do not forget my teaching,
But let your heart keep my commandments;
For length of days and years of life,
And peace they will add to you.
Do not let kindness and truth leave you;
Bind them around your neck,
Write them on the tablet of your heart.
So you will find favor and good repute
In the sight of God and man.
Trust in the Lord with all your heart,
And do not lean on your own understanding.
In all your ways acknowledge Him,
And He will make your paths straight.

Time to Do Good

We please our Lord when we use our time to do good works. Both the Old and New Testaments support this idea. Psalm 34:11-14 instructs us to depart from evil and pursue peace if we desire to see good throughout our length of days. First Peter 3:10-11 contains a very similar message. Both passages urge us to be peace-loving, self-controlled and benevolent. When we fulfill these commands, we honor our Lord with our time and glorify Him with our lives.

We can give our time to Jesus because He has given us so much. Our loving Savior offers us hope of salvation and calls us to a life of good works. We are blessed beyond imagination by our Lord, and we fulfill our greatest potential on earth when we give our time to serving in His kingdom.

Our benevolence should help people in the world, but giving our time to good deeds should begin at home. The virtuous woman of Proverbs 31 was a glory to her husband and family because of her wise use of time. Her good deeds blessed her entire household and endeared her to her family. Read verses 27-29:

She looks well to the ways of her household,
And does not eat the bread of idleness.
Her children rise up and bless her;
Her husband also, and he praises her, saying:
"Many daughters have done nobly,
But you excel them all."

Likewise, husbands are urged in Ecclesiastes 9:9 to make their wives a priority.

How different would our culture be today if husbands and wives seriously devoted themselves to their spouses and children? We could take the family off our society's endangered species list if we treasured time with our families. As Christian women, a great deal of our time is spent with our families in the privacy of our homes. It is here, secluded from the outside world, that we begin living out our Christianity.

Time to Grow

Our Lord also desires that we give our time to developing a personal relationship with Him. It is vital to our spiritual development that we both spend time in worship and fellowship with the saints and also that we give ourselves individually to Bible study and prayer. When our schedules are most hectic and deadlines threaten to crowd out time with God, this is when we need to commune with Him most. If we give Him our time, He will restore our serenity and help ease our burdens. Thus, we will find ourselves enriched and at peace. When we make spending time with our Lord a matter of first priority, we will reap the spiritual blessings that come from a closer walk with God.

Depriving ourselves of time with our Father will cause spiritual atrophy. Since his birth, doctors have charted my son Carson's growth to make sure he is healthy and strong. As his mother, I am attentive to his diet and physical progress. I must be even more vigilant, however, in encouraging his spiritual growth – and mine. All of us see the need for physical nourishment, but often we neglect to feed our souls. We forfeit much potential spiritual growth when we do not devote ourselves to Bible study and prayer.

Like Mary, we also should pause from time to time to simply experience God. "Be still, and know that I am God," reads Psalm 46:10 (NKJV). Often it is only in stillness that we are able to quiet restless spirits, unclutter our minds, and refresh our bodies. It is important that we stop on occasion simply to drink in the beauty of God's creation and savor the majesty of His power. The second verse of the familiar hymn "Take Time to Be Holy" extols us,

Take time to be holy, The world rushes on;
Spend much time in secret With Jesus alone.
Abiding in Jesus, Like Him thou shalt be;
Thy friends in thy conduct His likeness shall see.

Rushing endlessly through life and filling every moment of the day can leave us feeling spiritually depleted. Sometimes the greatest blessings come not from doing, but just from being.

The Time of Our Lives

"There is an appointed time for everything. And there is a time for every event under heaven," begins Ecclesiastes 3:1. Verses 1-8 of this chapter are perhaps the most familiar biblical passage about time. These verses cite times for birth and death, planting and uprooting, weeping and laughing, loving and hating; and on the passage goes describing the cycles of life. In our culture we are often taught to begrudge the aging process and to fight the passing of youth. However, God's plan does not teach us to dread growing older. In fact, as Christians we can rejoice in the spiritual growth and maturity that age will bring. If we focus on growing a little more spiritual every day, it is exciting to ponder how much closer to God we could be 20, 30 or even 50 years from now.

Ecclesiastes offers wise advice for us to heed in whatever stage of life we find ourselves. Ecclesiastes 12:1 urges,

Remember also your Creator in the days of your youth,
before the evil days come and the years draw near when
you will say, "I have no delight in them."

Encouraging our children and teenagers to give their time to the Lord is important for their spiritual growth as well as for the future of the church. Youth is the time to set priorities and goals, and it is an important period for laying spiritual foundations.

Adulthood brings independence and opportunity, but along with these come responsibility and accountability. Ecclesiastes 11:9 says,

[L]et your heart be pleasant during the days of young
manhood. And follow the impulses of your heart and the
desires of your eyes. Yet know that God will bring you
to judgment for all these things.

During these busy years, it is important to remain faithful to the work of the church. Career advancement and financial growth take a more significant role in adulthood, but we must remain vigilant throughout this stage of life to avoid crowding out our time with God. Adulthood is a prime time for building marriage relationships, rearing children, ministering to the needy and serving in the kingdom. The church needs vibrant, grounded adults who are committed to its growth.

Verse 10 reminds us that "childhood and the prime of life are fleeting." Old age comes quickly, and time can be a friend or foe in the golden years of life. By this time, children have been reared and retirement has come. This era is prime for increased service and spiritual growth. Failing health may limit some activities, but the Lord will always provide ways to serve if we are willing. With the spiritual maturity that should accompany age comes tremendous opportunity for influence. Children, grandchildren and young church members crave and value the wisdom and experience of mature Christians. The role of an older Christian should not diminish; this should be a fruitful time of teaching and giving.

No matter what stage of life we find ourselves in, this is the perfect time to give ourselves wholeheartedly in service to the Lord. Ecclesiastes 11:6 urges us, "Sow your seed in the morning, and do not be idle in the evening, for you do not know whether morning or evening sowing will succeed, or whether both of them alike will be good." We should never discount our abilities or leave tasks undone because of our age. It is important that throughout life, we leave enough flexibility in our schedules to respond to the Lord. Trying to give our time to God every day is a pledge worth keeping throughout life.

Giving on God's Time

Giving our time to God is an investment because His time is eternal. Our Creator and everlasting God existed before the world and even before time itself. Psalm 90:1-4, 12 exults,

> Lord, Thou hast been our dwelling place in all generations.
> Before the mountains were born,

Or Thou didst give birth to the earth and the world,
Even from everlasting to everlasting, Thou art God. ...
For a thousand years in Thy sight
Are like yesterday when it passes by,
Or as a watch in the night. ...
So teach us to number our days,
That we may present to Thee a heart of wisdom.

He who created the world is certainly able to fill our time with blessings when we are willing and eager to share it with Him.

In order to maintain a proper perspective of our time on earth, we must keep our eyes fixed on the world to come and the promise of heaven. Our days are numbered in this life, but God's promise to His children is life eternal. Our faithfulness and vigilance will not go unheeded by our Lord. Like Mary, if we determine to sit at the feet of Jesus in this life, joy will be ours as we take our places before the throne of God in heaven.

For What It's Worth

Psalm 144:4 reminds us, "Man is like a mere breath; His days are like a passing shadow." Although worldly concerns threaten to crowd out time spent in communion with God or service to others, giving our time to God is a matter of utmost importance. This is a challenge we will face throughout life. Like Mary, we must strive daily to keep our priorities in check. Whether we find ourselves in youth, adulthood or old age, now is the right time to serve the Lord. We must remember that although our days are numbered in this life, the Christian is not bound by the world's time. Life is fleeting, but God's time is eternal. When we give God our time, we will be fruitful and blessed in our walk with the Lord and learn more about giving for all it's worth.

Give an Answer

1. Read Luke 10:38-42. Contrast the attitudes of Mary and Martha.
2. What advice does Proverbs 3:1-6 give about our purpose in life? How would application of this passage affect our use of time?
3. What wisdom can we glean from Psalm 34:11-14 and 1 Peter 3:10-12?

4. To what two things does Psalm 144:4 compare the span of our lives?
5. When is the best time to serve the Lord, according to Ecclesiastes 11:6?
6. What does Psalm 90:1-4 teach us about God's perspective of time?

Give It Some Thought

1. How did Mary and Martha differ in their approaches to their encounter with Jesus in Luke 10:38-42? What lessons can we learn from this story?
2. How would today's families be impacted by an investment of time by spouses and parents?
3. Of what consequence is time spent in worship or fellowship with other Christians? How do prayer and Bible study impact spiritual growth?
4. Discuss the unique challenges and opportunities that accompany each stage in the cycle of life.
5. How can we maintain an eternal perspective of time and avoid crowding the Lord out of our schedules?

Give It a Try

1. Take a look at your calendar. Do planned activities of your congregation take precedence over other commitments? What would an outsider deduce about your priorities based on your schedule?
2. Set aside daily time to commune with God in prayer at a time of day when you are freshest. If that sounds impossible, try incorporating this devotional time into a regularly scheduled activity, such as your daily commute to work, an afternoon walk or evening chores.
3. Make daily Bible reading a family priority. Read a chapter or even a few verses at the dinner table, and discuss the passage's meaning over supper.

CHAPTER 8

A LOYAL FRIEND

"And one of the scribes ... asked Him, 'What commandment is the foremost of all?' Jesus answered, 'The foremost is, "Hear, O Israel! The Lord our God is one Lord; and you shall love the Lord your God with all your heart, and with all your soul, and with all your mind, and with all your strength." The second is this, "You shall love your neighbor as yourself." There is no other commandment greater than these' " (Mark 12:28-31).

The three women huddled close as they steeled themselves against the cool morning wind. They had walked to the edge of town in silence, too tired emotionally for the casual banter and easy laughter so typical of their relationship. Quiet though they were, they found a measure of comfort in just being together. Naomi looked briefly at her young companions, and fresh tears filled her eyes.

Naomi inhaled deeply as she surveyed for the last time the land she had inhabited for several years. She sighed wistfully, remembering the promise Moab had once held for her family. Along with her husband and two sons, she had left the famine of Bethlehem nearly a decade ago in search of a more abundant life. They had entered this land in springtime, welcomed by the verdant landscape. For many years their life in Moab was happy and blessed, but Naomi now saw her life mirrored in the stark, barren scenery before her.

Today Naomi would return to Judah, which meant parting with her two daughters-in-law. She had accepted and loved Orpah and Ruth like daughters, and she felt new grief as she pulled them close one final time. Both girls had pleaded to remain with Naomi, but she knew their place was in Moab with their families. Determined not to make their goodbyes even more difficult, Naomi struggled fiercely against the emotions that threatened her composure. Unwelcome tears blurred her vision, and she closed her eyes.

Before saying her final goodbyes, Orpah instinctively put her arm around her mother-in-law. She wondered fleetingly if the trip back to Judah would be too difficult for Naomi, but she knew that her mother-in-law was a woman of quiet strength. It pained her deeply to part with Naomi, but she knew the time had come. With a final kiss on the cheek, Orpah turned away as she wept bitterly. She could not bear to look back as she walked away.

Naomi loosened her embrace of Ruth, but Ruth clung tighter still. "Dear, sweet Ruth," Naomi thought to herself. "She has been both daughter and friend to me. How I will miss her meek and sensitive spirit." Against her desire Naomi gently pushed Ruth away. Straightening her posture, Naomi resolved to say goodbye. She searched the eyes of her daughter-in-law, expecting to find sadness and resignation, but instead she saw strength and determination. Something in Ruth's eyes told Naomi that their journey would not end here, after all.

Reading from the book of Ruth, we know that, in fact, Naomi and Ruth's journey was just beginning. Their relationship serves as a powerful example of friendship and loyalty. Our story opens in Chapter 1. After losing her husband and sons, Naomi determined to return to Judah, the land of her youth. She told her daughters-in-law in verse 8,

> Go, return each of you to her mother's house. May the Lord deal kindly with you as you have dealt with the dead and with me. May the Lord grant that you may find rest, each in the house of her husband.

Both Orpah and Ruth pleaded to stay with Naomi, but Naomi was swift to discourage them. At last, Orpah said farewell to her mother-in-law, but Ruth would not be persuaded. In verses 16-17, Ruth pledged her loyalty to Naomi:

> Do not urge me to leave you or turn back from following you; for where you go, I will go, and where you lodge, I will lodge. Your people shall be my people, and your God, my God. Where you die, I will die, and there I will be buried. Thus may the Lord do to me, and worse, if anything but death parts you and me.

Ruth accompanied Naomi back to Bethlehem, and the two arrived at the beginning of the barley harvest. Ruth went to glean in a field of reapers, and there she met Boaz, a kinsman of Elimelech. News of Ruth's sacrifices for Naomi had reached his ears, and he was touched by her faithfulness. Boaz was kind and generous to Ruth. Ruth ultimately married Boaz and had a son. Ruth 4:14-15 says,

> Then the women said to Naomi, "Blessed is the Lord who has not left you without a redeemer today, and may his name become famous in Israel. May he also be to you a restorer of life and a sustainer of your old age; for your daughter-in-law, who loves you and is better to you than seven sons, has given birth to him."

Consider the agony Naomi must have experienced having to bury her husband and both sons within a few years. Suddenly, she became a foreigner in a strange land. The journey from Moab back to Judah would have been more than 100 miles. How frightening this pilgrimage would have been for a woman traveling with little money and no protector. She must have felt lonely as she prepared to part with her daughters-in-law. Naomi was obviously a godly woman and a kind mother-in-law because both Orpah and Ruth pleaded to remain with her. Orpah ultimately parted with Naomi, but Ruth stood by her.

How thankful Naomi must have been for dear, loyal Ruth. What a friend Ruth was to her mother-in-law. Still a young woman, Ruth was willing to give up potential happiness with a new Moabite husband in order to care for Naomi. Her pledge to Naomi in Ruth 1:16-17, often repeated in weddings, is a beautiful statement of love and devotion. Ruth kept her promise, willingly leaving her family, friends and native country to accompany Naomi back to Judah. She braved a new culture without hesitation or complaint.

While in Judah, Ruth worked diligently to provide food for her mother-in-law and herself. Throughout everything, she never wavered in her faithfulness or sought pity for her sacrifice. A foreigner who could have been ostracized, Ruth's humility and kindness won respect and admiration in Bethlehem. Naomi must have appreciated her daughter-in-law's companionship. Knowing Ruth's esteem for her must have given her purpose and encouragement during a time of tremendous upheaval.

God rewarded Ruth's faithfulness by allowing her to marry Boaz and blessing their union with a son. The baby, Obed, ultimately found his place in the lineage of Jesus as the father of Jesse and grandfather of David. Because Ruth was willing to give up potential happiness for herself to care for her mother-in-law, she found herself loved and blessed in her new land. The Lord remembered and rewarded her sacrificial attitude. Ruth gave by offering herself in friendship and loyalty to Naomi. Her example of faithfulness still inspires us today.

Loyal to Our Lord

When asked by a scribe which commandment was the greatest, Jesus replied in Mark 12:29-31,

> The foremost is, "Hear, O Israel! The Lord our God is one Lord; and you shall love the Lord your God with all your heart, and with all your soul, and with all your mind, and with all your strength." The second is this, "You shall love your neighbor as yourself." There is no other commandment greater than these.

Loving God and loving our neighbors go hand in hand, and to do either fully we must do both.

As we strive to develop the qualities of loyalty and friendship, let us look first to God. Before lunch one day, Carson led our prayer. He clasped his hands, bowed his head and began, "Dear God ... ." He sat, deep in thought, for several minutes. Finally he said, "We would like for You to watch cartoons and movies with us. Amen." What a sweet invitation! How humbling it is to realize that in one sentence, my 2-year-old expressed more sense of companionship with our Lord than I have in a lifetime of prayers. Often we ask the Lord to be with us as our Protector, our Redeemer or our Provider, but how often do we ask Him just to be with us?

Consider the camaraderie described in the first and third stanzas of the hymn "My God and I":

> My God and I go in the fields together,
> We walk and talk as good friends should and do;
> We clasp our hands, our voices ring with laughter,

My God and I walk through the meadows hue ... .
My God and I will go for aye together,
We'll walk and talk as good friends should and do;
This earth will pass, and with it common trifles,
But God and I will go unendingly ... .

Joy will be ours when we walk through life hand in hand with our Lord.

Through prayer, we are able to draw close to our Lord. Talking to Him will strengthen our friendship and help us trust His sovereignty in our lives. Being loyal to our Lord also means reading His Word, obeying His commands and speaking for Truth. Our faithfulness to God will strengthen our fellow Christians and give the world a godly example. If as Christians we stand together for the Lord, we will grow spiritually and influence the world for good.

Our Lord deserves our faithfulness because He is faithful. Second Timothy 2:13 explains, "If we are faithless, He remains faithful; for He cannot deny Himself." God cannot deny His character; His loyalty is eternal. We can always count on our heavenly Father, who will never leave us. Although we might turn our faces from the Lord from time to time or forget His constant presence, He will remain faithful. He will never forsake us, overlook us or break His promises. Hebrews 10:23 urges, "Let us hold fast the confession of our hope without wavering, for He who promised is faithful."

Forever Friends

Being a friend to God also means loving our neighbors as ourselves. Our loyalty to other people is often expressed through friendship. Even in our fast-paced, materialistic culture, people in our world still realize that true friendship is a rare gift. Samuel Taylor Coleridge called friendship "a sheltering tree"; Woodrow Wilson, "the only cement that will hold the world together"; and Lord Byron, "Love without his wings." Consider this passage about the value of friendship by Andrew M. Greeley, as quoted in *A Friend Is Someone Special*:

There is an electricity about a friendship relationship. We are both more relaxed and more sensitive, more creative and more reflective, more energetic and more casual, more excited and more serene. It is as though when we come in contact with our friend we enter into a different environment (C.R. Gibson, 1975, p. 18).

Friends bring joy and laughter to our world; their presence in our lives makes our joys brighter and our worries lighter.

As Christians, the friendships that we share in the family of God go much deeper than relationships shared by people in the world. While friendships in the world may be casual and superficial, our relationships with fellow Christians have their roots in eternal principles. Our unity in Christ gives us a shared peace, a shared purpose and a shared promise. Even when we first meet, right away we can experience camaraderie and kinship because of our shared focus. As members of the Lord's church, we find ourselves edified and strengthened by our brothers and sisters in Christ. As side by side we worship and work together, we are able to help each other grow and flourish in the kingdom of God.

For most of us, friendships have blossomed and faded through the years. In our transient age, many people come into our lives for a season. Relationships based solely on shared circumstances or activities come and go, but our most treasured friendships endure. The relationships that span separations of time and distance are most often those with our Christian sisters. When reunited, no matter how long we have been apart, the special bonds we share allow us to pick back up as if no time has passed. Thinking of these dear friends makes our hearts smile and gives us courage to face difficult days.

Just as Naomi needed Ruth for her pilgrimage back to Judah, we need the support of other Christians in our spiritual journey. Our loving Father knows this and makes provisions for us in His church. The blessings we experience through friendship and fellowship with other Christians have been ordained by God. Our Lord desires and commands that we give friendship to each other. Jesus said in John 15:12-14,

> This is My commandment, that you love one another, just as I have loved you. Greater love has no one than this, that one lay down his life for his friends. You are My friends, if you do what I command you.

The type of friendship described here is loyal and true. Christ made the ultimate sacrifice for us by giving us His life. Most of us will never be called to give our lives for our friends, but we certainly will be called time and time again to give them our hearts. We please and honor our Lord when we extend ourselves in love and fellowship to those around us. Our loyalty to God is often expressed in our propensity to love other people.

Friends of God's Children

Romans 12:10-18 gives wise counsel in how we are to give ourselves in loyalty and friendship to fellow Christians:

> Be devoted to one another in brotherly love; give preference to one another in honor; not lagging behind in diligence, fervent in spirit, serving the Lord; rejoicing in hope, persevering in tribulation, devoted to prayer, contributing to the needs of the saints, practicing hospitality (vv. 10-13).

Who would not want to be part of a church family with these characteristics? The congregation described here is loving, generous, encouraging and welcoming. Imagine the spiritual growth our congregations would experience if outsiders saw these characteristics consistently displayed among our members.

Truly, our church buildings would overflow if the world could see us heeding Jesus' words in John 13:35: "By this all men will know that you are My disciples, if you have love for one another." First Corinthians 13:4-7, a well-known and often-quoted passage, depicts what love looks like: patient, kind, meek, forgiving and sincere. Putting this passage into practice would greatly impact our world for the cause of Christ.

Emulating Christ's love for the church in cultivating relationships with fellow Christians entails more than casual contact and superficial interaction. As God's children, we should demonstrate the same care and interest for each other as we would for our own brothers and sisters.

When we determine to devote ourselves to living in harmony with our fellow Christians, our churches will experience growth and we will reap the spiritual blessings described in Galatians 5:22-

23: "But the fruit of the Spirit is love, joy, peace, patience, kindness, goodness, faithfulness, gentleness, self-control; against such things there is no law." Giving our hearts to our fellow Christians in friendship and loyalty is certainly a goal worth striving for.

The Journey
by Melissa Lester

Many roads – winding, twisting, wandering – con-
    verging here.
For one brief moment in a lifetime of moments, we
    will journey together.
Arm in arm we will laugh and sing, growing as we
    bask in the warmth and security of friendship.
Cherished memories, like flowers, will bloom in the
    meadows of our innocence.
Under the eye of the moon we will share secrets
    and silent tears.
We will splash and play in the waters of our youth
    – each shimmering drop a dream of what is yet
    to be.
If there be rocks in your path and you should stum-
    ble, I will catch you.
If your path grows dark and you tremble with fear, I
    will hold your hand in mine and my light will be
    also yours.
And if you should stray from the path and lose your
    way, I will call your name and you will be found.
In these days we will gather roses and I will call you
    friend.
And when these days are over and the sun has set
    on youth, I know not where our paths will lead us.
But in times of trouble, sorrow and remembrance, I
    have only to look into my heart and I will find
    you.
My heart will take me back to the path we walked
    together.
The air will smell as sweet, and the wind will echo
    the joy and laughter of more carefree days.
The flowers I carry from my youth will remind me

of our times together, their fragrance of the love
we shared.

You in your corner of the world and I in mine have
only to remember our days together,

And our hearts will bridge the distance to bring us
back to this place of peace, love and unending
friendship.

And when I survey my life's journey, I will think of
you and my heart will smile.

I will know that my path has been easier, my load
lighter, and that I am better for having traveled
with you.

For What It's Worth

Giving ourselves in loyalty and friendship to God and other people is our charge as Christians. As Jesus told a scribe in Mark 12,
the first commandment for each of us is to love God with all our
hearts, minds and strength; the second is to love our neighbors as
ourselves. In the story of Ruth, we find a beautiful example of love
and devotion. Ruth honored the Lord through her faithfulness to
her mother-in-law. She was willing to leave her family and the only
land she had ever known in order to accompany Naomi to Judah.
Loyal and kind, Ruth was richly blessed because of her godly life
choices. We, too, should stand firm for the Lord and His children.
God will reward our faithfulness to Him, and we will be encouraged and strengthened by our relationships cultivated with fellow
Christians. Our friendships with God and our brothers and sisters
in Christ are truly the best gifts we can give ourselves.

Give an Answer

1. How long did Ruth pledge to be faithful to her mother-in-law
   in Ruth 1:16-17?
2. What is the posture of the faithful Christian as described in
   Ephesians 6:14-16?
3. Read 2 Timothy 2:11-13. How can we be assured of God's faithfulness?

4. How does our treatment of other people reflect our relationship with Christ according to John 15:12-14?
5. Describe how we are to treat our brothers and sisters in Christ as commanded in Romans 12:10-18.
6. What qualities are found in loving relationships as described in 2 Corinthians 13:4-7?

Give It Some Thought

1. What obstacles make us stumble in our relationships with Christ?
2. How would you describe the love and faithfulness of God to someone who does not know Him?
3. Describe a time when you were blessed by the love and friendship of a Christian sister.
4. Think back over the friendships that have blossomed and faded in your life. What similarities do you find in the relationships that have grown stronger over time?
5. How do we experience the faithfulness of God through our relationships with fellow Christians?

Give It a Try

1. Nurture your relationship with a Christian sister through planning a lunch date, movie night or shopping excursion.
2. Think about a special friend from your youth with whom you have lost contact, and set aside time for a phone call or visit.
3. A quote from Samuel Johnson reads, "We cannot tell the precise moment when friendship is formed. As in filling a vessel drop by drop, there is at last a drop which makes it run over; so in a series of kindnesses there is at last one which makes the heart run over." Print this passage on the front of an invitation for a "friendship tea." Invite a few guests, and instruct each one to bring another friend whom you have not met. Over tea and conversation, you will have opportunity to read scriptures about friendship and make new acquaintances.

CHAPTER 9

PLANTING SEEDS FOR THE KINGDOM

"But the goal of our instruction is love from a pure heart and a good conscience and a sincere faith" (1 Timothy 1:5).

Jovial sounds rang out among disciples still lingering after gathering for worship in Ephesus. Relieved from being quiet and still, children scampered about noisily, their boundless energy evident as they meandered happily through groups of mingling adults. Fields ready to be planted beckoned, but the good weather and friendly banter made it difficult to part. On a lovely day like this, it might be hours before the crowd of saints would dwindle.

Near the edge of the assembly, a young woman peered hopefully into the crowd. "Oh, there she is," an elderly man directed, pointing toward a group of women clustered under the shade of a sycamore tree. The young woman's gaze settled on a tall, auburn-haired woman who appeared to be telling a story. Laughter broke out among the women surrounding her as she smiled and gestured animatedly.

The young woman quietly approached the group, a ruddy-faced little boy in tow. At last the group dispersed and the young woman stepped forward. "Priscilla?" she asked expectantly.

"Yes," the woman replied, absent-mindedly fingering a handful of seeds one of the ladies had brought. She knew Aquila was eager to get to his garden before daylight faded.

"Oh, thank you, thank you," the young woman said, her eyes filling with tears as she hugged this woman she had so long wanted to meet.

Surprised by this reaction, Priscilla dropped a few of the seeds. She looked questioningly into the faces of the young woman and the small boy who peered at her coyly from behind his mother's skirt. "Do I know you, dear?" Priscilla asked.

"Oh, I'm sorry," the young woman stammered, a bit embarrassed at her sudden tears and impetuous display of affection. "I am Miriam, and this is my son, Joshua. My husband, Eli, and I traveled here from Achaia. Several years ago we were taught the gospel by Apollos. Our family and many others learned about the Messiah from Apollos. He spoke so often of you and your husband – of how you studied with him and taught him the way of God more fully. Eli was once a Pharisee, but he is now teaching other Jews about Jesus. I just wanted you to know how much good you and your husband have done."

Incredulous at what she was hearing, Priscilla's eyes filled with tears. She and Aquila had studied with Apollos, but she had never contemplated how far-reaching the effects of their time with him might be. As she stared into the faces of Miriam and Joshua, at once she felt honored and humbled to know the Lord had used her to spread the good news. "To God be the glory," she said at last.

Miriam and Priscilla chatted like old friends reunited until from across the crowd a young man caught Miriam's eye and motioned that it was time to leave. The two women said their goodbyes, and Miriam and Joshua joined Eli to continue their journey.

Now alone under the sycamore tree, Priscilla examined her handful of seeds. "Thank You, Father," she prayed, "that even the smallest seeds we plant for Your sake can become great. Please give me hunger for Your Word, wisdom to understand, zeal to teach, and eagerness to share Your love so that I may never miss an opportunity to plant seeds for Your kingdom."

This scene between Priscilla and a woman taught by Apollos, although not described in the Bible, is easy to imagine. Many people were brought to the Lord because of seeds planted by Priscilla and her husband, Aquila. Over the years their paths must have crossed with many people converted to Christianity because of their efforts. Their hearts must have leapt with joy knowing the gospel was spread throughout Asia in part because of their willingness to teach with boldness and love.

We are first introduced to Priscilla, later called Prisca, in Acts 18. Verses 1-2 tell us that she and Aquila went to Corinth when Claudius expelled all Jews from Rome. Tent makers by trade, in Corinth they met and opened their home to Paul. Paul began teaching the Jews in Corinth about the Messiah. In a vision the Lord urged Paul, "Do not be afraid any longer, but go on speaking and do not be silent; for I am with you, and no man will attack you in order to harm you, for I have many people in this city" (vv. 9-10).

During the year and a half Paul spent in Corinth, he taught the gospel to many Jews, including the leader of the synagogue. Finally called before the judgment seat and driven from Corinth by angry Jews, Paul set sail for Syria along with Aquila and Priscilla. Paul stopped in Ephesus, where he left Aquila and Priscilla, before continuing his journey.

Paul held this couple in high regard and continued his relationship with them after they parted company. They had proven to be capable teachers and faithful comrades despite trials and persecution. He referred to them in letters to the churches in Corinth and Rome and also in a letter to Timothy. "Greet Prisca and Aquila, my fellow workers in Christ Jesus, who for my life risked their own necks," he urged in Romans 16:3-4. He wrote in 1 Corinthians 16:19, "The churches of Asia greet you. Aquila and Prisca greet you heartily in the Lord, with the church that is in their house." "Greet Prisca and Aquila," he urged in 2 Timothy 4:19.

In Ephesus, Aquila and Priscilla met Apollos. Apollos is described in Acts 18:24 as eloquent and mighty in the Scriptures. Verses 25-26 tell us,

> This man had been instructed in the way of the Lord; and being fervent in spirit, he was speaking and teaching accurately the things concerning Jesus, being acquainted only with the baptism of John; and he began to speak out boldly in the synagogue. But when Priscilla and Aquila heard him, they took him aside and explained to him the way of God more accurately.

Apollos became a great missionary, bringing countless Jews to Christ throughout his life. First, we are told that in Achaia "he helped greatly those who had believed through grace; for he powerfully refuted the Jews in public, demonstrating by the Scriptures that Jesus was the Christ" (Acts 18:27-28). He is also mentioned in passages in 1 Corinthians and Titus. In regard to the church at Corinth, Paul said, "I planted, Apollos watered, but God was causing the growth" (1 Corinthians 3:6). He urged Titus in Titus 3:13, "Diligently help Zenas the lawyer and Apollos on their way so that nothing is lacking for them."

As Christian women, we have a powerful example in Priscilla of one woman's ability to encourage and motivate those around her. She may never have graced a pulpit or addressed large groups in the synagogue, but the impact of Priscilla's teaching was far-reaching. She probably would have been awed to realize how many people she helped lead to the Lord. As a result of her diligent study and godly example, she proved to be a powerful influence in the lives of Paul, Apollos and countless other Jews of her time. And although she has not walked this earth for nearly 2,000 years, through the biblical account of her life, Priscilla is still teaching us today.

We can learn several lessons from Priscilla. First, we can assume that she was a serious student of God's Word. How spiritually rich the year and a half she and Aquila spent with Paul in Corinth must have been. Lively discussions, ardent prayers and sincere praises must have filled their home as they worked and studied together. Obviously, Priscilla had more than a cursory knowledge of the gospel because she was able to expound on the knowledge of Apollos, a learned Jew.

Second, she was eager to share her knowledge. We can deduce that she took an active role in teaching Apollos because her name is listed before her husband's in the description of their encounter in Acts 18. She could have taken a back seat in teaching and relied on Aquila's knowledge and abilities, but she resolved to do her part as well.

Third, she looked for teachable moments. A busy wife and business woman, Priscilla easily could have let other priorities come before teaching Apollos, yet she made time to study with him.

Fourth, she was brave enough to share the good news. By sharing their faith, she and Aquila risked rejection from Apollos – or worse. Considering the religious climate of the day, teaching about the Messiah would have brought certain persecution, yet this faithful couple willingly put themselves in harm's way in order to spread the gospel.

Finally, Priscilla's efforts were motivated by love. She and Aquila did not seek to humiliate Apollos by confronting him in the synagogue. Instead, Scripture tells us they taught him privately. No doubt, her sincerity and humility made Apollos more open to learning the truth. She touched countless people both directly and indirectly because of her love for the Lord and concern for the lost. The precious souls she taught grew in their love for the Lord and were motivated to teach more people, who would in turn teach more people. Priscilla's sincere, compassionate nature endeared her to Christians throughout Asia and encouraged the spiritual development of countless people.

Priscilla gives us a powerful example of what God can do with the small seeds one person plants in His name. As Christian women who are eager to teach, we face opportunities every day to plant seeds that will bring about spiritual growth today and a glorious harvest in eternity. Let us look to Scripture to learn how we are to excel in this grace of giving.

Prepared to Answer

Even though princes sit and talk against me, Thy
　servant meditates on Thy statutes.
Thy testimonies also are my delight; they are my
　counselors.
My soul cleaves to the dust; Revive me according to
　Thy word.
I have told of my ways, and Thou hast answered
　me; Teach me Thy statutes.
Make me understand the way of Thy precepts, so I
　will meditate on Thy wonders.
　　　　　　　　　　　　　　　　– Psalm 119:23-27

How will we ever be able to teach God's will if we are not earnest students of it ourselves? "My people are destroyed for lack of knowledge," laments Hosea 4:6. Sadly, this Old Testament verse still rings true in the church of our Lord today. Truth be told, many of us probably recall less about Bible events and characters than we did when we were children; and worse, we may not have enough Bible knowledge to articulate, explain or defend our beliefs from a scriptural basis. Relying on the knowledge or faith of other people will not negate our responsibilities in the kingdom of God. Studying the Bible, as a body and as individuals, is an essential part of our spiritual development. When we neglect to feed our minds the meat of God's Word, spiritual atrophy is inevitable. "For though by this time you ought to be teachers," scolds Hebrews 5:12, "you have need again for someone to teach you the elementary principles of the oracles of God, and you have come to need milk and not solid food."

Reaching spiritual maturity is a goal that will be met only with persistence. Consider the focus on God's precepts described in Deuteronomy:

> And these words ... shall be on your heart; and you shall teach them diligently to your sons and shall talk of them when you sit in your house and when you walk by the way and when you lie down and when you rise up. And you shall bind them as a sign on your hand and they shall be as frontals on your forehead. And you shall write them on the doorposts of your house and on your gates (6:6-9).

The attitude described here toward the Word of God is not casual or passive, as many in our day would like their Christianity to be. We must strive to become like little children again in our spiritual walk, never tiring of learning about the wonders of our Father. He desires that we have hunger for His Word, diligence to dig deeply into Scripture, and tender hearts to receive His instruction.

Truly, the most difficult part of studying the Bible is opening the Book and getting started. Our reward is great, however, when we do. When we commit ourselves to studying God's Word, we will find within its pages love, joy, peace, guidance, understanding and hope. When we consider the Author of the Bible and the message it contains, it is shameful and incomprehensible that we could ever lose our hunger for it. The Creator of the universe and all that is in it has given us an instruction manual for life. He has written us a passionate love letter that details a love so deep and wide it goes beyond the scope of human comprehension. The depth and wisdom of the Bible is unsurpassed by any other book ever written. Amazingly, even passages read many times reveal new insights when explored again.

The spiritual blessings we experience when we spend time with our Lord are many. Our time with Him will make us more compassionate, more humble, more content, more joyful and more holy. When we dig deeply into God's Word, we will be spiritually filled and able to heed Paul's instruction in 2 Timothy 2:15: "Study to shew thyself approved unto God, a workman that needeth not to be ashamed, rightly dividing the word of truth" (KJV).

Ready to Teach

Lack of biblical knowledge can make us shy away from teaching, but even the most profound Bible scholar can feel intimidated when it comes to telling others about Christ. When we encounter opportunities to share our faith, often our throats tighten and our hearts beat faster. Myriad doubts about our abilities surface: "What should I say?" we ask ourselves. "What if I say the wrong thing? I might offend her or sound like a religious fanatic. What if she thinks I'm overstepping my bounds or just being judgmental?" These periods of self-doubt may cause us to let teachable moments pass.

Fears about our knowledge or abilities in regard to teaching put a heavy weight on our shoulders – one that our Father does not expect us to bear. Consider the reassurance He gave a great leader of the Old Testament who early on expressed doubts about his qualifications. Moses described himself as "slow of speech and slow of tongue," but the Lord said to him in Exodus 4:11-12,

> Who has made man's mouth? Or who makes him dumb or deaf, or seeing or blind? Is it not I, the Lord? Now then go, and I, even I, will be with your mouth, and teach you what you are to say.

When we focus on our inadequacies as teachers, we forget that we can rely on our Father to guide us in what to say. When faced with an opportunity to share your faith, remember Jesus' words to His disciples in Luke 12:11-12:

> And when they bring you before the synagogues and
> the rulers and the authorities, do not become anxious
> about how or what you should speak in your defense, or
> what you should say; for the Holy Spirit will teach you
> in that very hour what you ought to say.

Our teaching should direct people to God and His Word, not our
own opinions. Therefore, we need not worry about not having all
the answers. God does, and that is all that matters.

Sometimes our hesitancy to teach might reveal doubts about the
power of our message to convict the hearts of those we teach.
Despite Jonah's failures in fleeing from God's command to go to
Nineveh, I have always at least admired the esteem he held for the
power of the message. He did not want to go to Nineveh because
he knew that if the people of this wicked city heard the message
of God, they would repent and be spared. He was angered when
God showed mercy on the city:

> And he prayed to the Lord and said, "Please Lord, was
> not this what I said while I was still in my own coun-
> try? Therefore, in order to forestall this I fled to Tarshish,
> for I knew that Thou art a gracious and compassionate
> God, slow to anger and abundant in lovingkindness, and
> one who relents concerning calamity" (Jonah 4:2).

Often we are tempted to look for ways to package the Word of
God in such a way that it will be more attractive or more palatable,
but watering down the good news will not bring more people to
Christ. The simple, unadorned, enduring message of salvation is
one that every person who has ever walked the earth needs to hear
and heed. God's Word has the power to awaken sleeping con-
sciences, mend broken hearts, heal wounded spirits, fill empty
lives, and save lost souls. His message is powerful; all we have to
do is share it.

Fields to Plant

Women today have so many opportunities to teach. Some women
have been disheartened by focusing solely on 1 Timothy 2:11-12
in regard to teaching: "Let a woman quietly receive instruction
with entire submissiveness. But I do not allow a woman to teach

or exercise authority over a man, but to remain quiet." As Christian women, we have not been given biblical authority to preach to men or to usurp authority from our brothers in Christ; but there are so many other areas where we are called to serve. Rather than feeling disgruntled or deflated about what we cannot do, let us look instead at all that we can do. Let us strive to be like Ezra, who "had set his heart to study the law of the Lord, and to practice it, and to teach His statutes and ordinances in Israel" (Ezra 7:10). If we are willing to plant seeds in the kingdom of God, we will find opportunities every day to sow seeds in places and in people that others would overlook. Perhaps you will find here a field ready to be planted, young plants eager to be watered, or a neglected garden in need of tender pruning.

• *In the Home.* As daughters, sisters, wives, mothers, aunts, grandmothers and cousins, we have opportunities to model service, faithfulness and compassion to our families. It is easy to look into the world for opportunities to share God's love while neglecting to feed spiritually those closest to us. Before we look beyond our homes and families, however, we must examine the kind of teachers we are to those who know us most intimately. In particular, we are responsible for cultivating faith and faithfulness in our children. Psalm 78:4-7 declares,

> We will not conceal them from their children,
> But tell to the generation to come the praises of the
>   Lord,
> And His strength and His wondrous works that He
>   has done. …
> That the generation to come might know, even the
>   children yet to be born,
> That they may arise and tell them to their children,
> That they should put their confidence in God,
> And not forget the works of God,
> But keep His commandments.

We must work to preserve and pass on our love for the Lord. This duty is shared by mothers, grandmothers, aunts and others of influence. Consider Timothy, whose faith was nurtured by his mother and grandmother (2 Timothy 1:5).

• *In Ladies Bible Class.* Time spent studying the Bible with other women can be so spiritually enriching. In all my experiences with ladies Bible classes, I have found women to be wise, emotionally responsive and insightful in their approach to God's Word. There is truly no better way to draw closer to sisters in Christ than to spend time together sharing struggles, nurturing each other's faith, singing praises and approaching the throne of God in prayer. Titus 2:3-5 extols,

> Older women likewise are to be reverent in their behavior, not malicious gossips, nor enslaved to much wine, teaching what is good, that they may encourage the young women to love their husbands, to love their children, to be sensible, pure, workers at home, kind, being subject to their own husbands, that the word of God may not be dishonored.

The prospect of teaching an adult Bible class, even among friends, can be intimidating for some women. Most of us have not been socialized to feel comfortable leading in such a way. Taking the challenge, however, will bring many spiritual blessings. Rather than taking the role of lecturer, some women might find serving as a discussion leader more comfortable. Reading a passage of Scripture and then posing a variety of thought questions might be a good way to start. Many ladies Bible class books are available, as well, to help guide discussion. If your congregation does not have a ladies class, talk about the possibility with your sisters; you might find a group of ladies who are hungry to study together if only someone will take the lead.

• *In a Small-Group Bible Study.* Opening your home on a weekly or biweekly basis to teenagers, college students, young married couples, seniors or a cross-section of families in your congregation could be a wonderful way to experience lively Bible discussion and fellowship. Like Aquila and Priscilla, you and your husband can both contribute to the dialogue. Hosting or taking part in a small-group Bible study might prove to be a wonderful way to enrich your personal Bible study as well as get to know fellow Christians on a more intimate level.

• *Through Personal Evangelism.* Sometimes called "friendship evangelism," this type of teaching does not have to be as intimidating as it sounds. Simply looking for teachable moments with friends, neighbors and co-workers might open your eyes to opportunities to share your faith. The first step of personal evangelism is reaching out to those around us. Showing sincere interest, demonstrating compassion, helping meet needs, and serving faithfully will tell people about our faith even before we speak about it. Simply being a friend to the people we meet will make it easier to introduce them to our best friend, Jesus.

• *By Taking Part in Mission Trips.* Mark 16:15 commands us to "Go into all the world and preach the gospel to all creation." Whether we travel to another town or to another country, sharing the good news will allow us to teach others and grow spiritually. Quite often the person most altered by a mission trip is the one who goes. After a mission trip to Panama a few years ago, my father responded to the invitation his first Sunday back at home. As the minister for the congregation, his heartfelt confession came as a surprise to all. Seeing firsthand the hardships facing his Panamanian brethren, he felt challenged to move beyond what he felt had become comfortable Christianity. Experiencing the spiritual richness of a people so materially poor inspired him to study more, pray more, give more and serve more.

• *By Helping with Correspondence Courses.* Although not usually given much attention, this ministry is one that can introduce many people to the Lord. A Christian sister named Gracie takes very seriously her role of mailing and grading correspondence courses. She sincerely cares for all of her students and is a faithful correspondent, often including notes of encouragement with graded lessons.

• *Through Teaching Children.* I imagine that many of the most beloved people in heaven will be Bible teachers who helped put little souls on the path to heaven. These committed individuals endear themselves to children as they teach them fundamental truths and help them learn to love the Lord. Before he was even 2 years old, the high points of Carson's week were times spent in "Bible tass." It thrilled my soul to see him clasp his hands to pray and to hear him sing "Jesus Loves Me" with such delight. I am thankful for the women who give their time to help him learn about the wonders of God. "Jesus said, 'Let the little children come to me, and do not hinder them, for the kingdom of heaven belongs to such as these' " (Matthew 19:14 NIV). What wonderful blessings must be reserved for the women who gently, faithfully take small children by the hand and lead them to the Lord.

• *Through Writing.* Whether through writing magazine articles, Bible class books, Bible school curriculum or even personal correspondence, putting pen to paper can be a wonderful way for women to instruct, edify and exhort others. A blessing of the written word is its timelessness. Helpful passages can be tucked away and reread many times. If you would like to cultivate your writing abilities, keeping a journal of inspiration gained through personal Bible study might be a nice place to start. Whether you choose to share it with anyone else, when you finish you will have a priceless study reference for yourself.

• *By Personal Example.* "The blossom cannot tell what becomes of its odor, and no man can tell what becomes of his influence and example that roll away from him and go beyond his view." This anonymous quote beautifully illustrates the power of our example. We have all heard that our actions speak louder than our words, but sometimes we don't realize just how great the impact of our choices can be.

While a psychology major in college, my sister, Jennifer, took part in an internship program that involved working with troubled children. One particular little girl made a lasting impression. In her short life, this child had been abandoned by her natural parents and bounced from one foster home to another. She had several times run away from home only to be discovered going door to door looking for her mother.

In working with this little girl, Jennifer's patience wore thin and she often felt at a loss as to what to do next. She had to restrain the girl several times to keep her from acting out violently against the other children. As her internship drew to a close, Jennifer felt discouraged that she had not been able to help this little girl. She was disheartened until at their last session the little girl shyly revealed to the group that she loved Jennifer because she was so kind and gentle. She would make a wonderful mother one day, the little girl believed.

Jennifer cried recounting this story to me, realizing that she had made a difference after all. We can never fully know the impact we have on the people around us. Even for a troubled little girl with painful life experiences, seeing God's love displayed in a life lived with compassion and empathy can make a lasting impression.

Love to Teach

A quote from *Apples of Gold* reads, "To learn and never be filled is wisdom; to teach and never be weary is love" (C.R. Gibson, Norwalk, Conn., 1962; p. 14). Truly, teaching others about Christ is a ministry of love. In order to be pleasing to our Lord and effective in sharing His message, our words must come from a pure place. Like Priscilla, we must wrap our message in gentleness, humility and compassion. The Bible gives us some direction as to how we are to teach.

• *We are to be bold, yet gentle in our approach.* "[S]anctify Christ as Lord in your hearts, always being ready to make a defense to everyone who asks you to give an account for the hope that is in you, yet with gentleness and reverence" (1 Peter 3:15 NASB). We should be eager to share our faith, yet patient and tender in our delivery.

• *We are to model what we teach.* "[Y]ou, therefore, who teach another, do you not teach yourself? You who preach that one should not steal, do you steal?" (Romans 2:21). If people see that we are not genuine in the way we live, our hypocrisy will mar our positive influence and can overshadow any good we have done. We must deal honestly with our shortcomings and strive to walk in integrity. As humans, we know we will not achieve perfection, but together we can strive to become more like Christ.

• *Our lives should speak more eloquently than our words.* "[I]n speech, conduct, love, faith and purity, show yourself an example of those who believe" (1 Timothy 4:12). We must remember that we are ambassadors for Christ. As we go through our days – even in our briefest, most anonymous encounters – we should strive to carry ourselves in such a way that people would not be surprised to learn that we are Christians. When people see joy, compassion, humility and peace in us, it will be easier for us to teach them. When we let our lives shine for the Lord, people will gravitate toward the Christ they see in us.

• *We are to demonstrate genuine concern for those we teach.* "Do not sharply rebuke an older man, but rather appeal to him as a father, to the younger men as brothers, the older women as mothers, and the younger women as sisters, in all purity" (1 Timothy 5:1-2). If we love the lost as we love our brothers and sisters, our task will be so much easier. The faith of those we teach must be nurtured lovingly in order for it to grow and flourish.

• *Our motivation must be pure.* "But the goal of our instruction is love from a pure heart and a good conscience and a sincere faith" (1 Timothy 1:5). Our reasons for teaching must be God-approved. Our motivation must not be to elevate ourselves or put others down. The goal of our instruction must be to elevate Christ and to help others draw closer to Him, so that those we teach can experience the love, contentment and faith described in 1 Timothy 1:5.

• *Saving souls, not winning debates, must be our focus.* "And the Lord's bond-servant must not be quarrelsome, but be kind to all, able to teach, patient when wronged, with gentleness correcting those who are in opposition, if perhaps God may grant them repentance leading to the knowledge of the truth, and they may come to their senses and escape from the snare of the devil, having been held captive by him to do his will" (2 Timothy 2:24-26).

We must remember what is at stake when we are teaching lost souls: their salvation, not our pride. We will not argue, debate or berate people into heaven. We must take the time to teach them with compassion and gentleness. Eternal life hangs in the balance.

For What It's Worth

"Teachers touch the future," a popular saying suggests. I would extend that quote to say that godly teachers touch eternity. Through Bible study, we increase our knowledge and holiness; through teaching we help other people come to know the love of our Father. Like Priscilla, we must learn to share our faith in a way that is bold, yet gentle. Looking for people to teach and opening our eyes to teachable moments will allow us to minister powerfully to the people in our lives. Opportunities abound to share the love of Christ if we are willing. Proverbs 9:9-10 counsels,

Give instruction to a wise man, and he will be still wiser, Teach a righteous man, and he will increase his learning. The fear of the Lord is the beginning of wisdom, And the knowledge of the Holy One is understanding.

Becoming students of God's Word and teaching others about Jesus are vital to our spiritual growth. Through our giving, we can plant seeds that, with God's blessing, will bring about spiritual growth today and a glorious harvest in eternity.

Give an Answer

1. What did Apollos learn from his meeting with Priscilla and Aquila (Acts 18:24-26)?
2. What does Hebrews 5:12 reveal about the importance of Bible study?
3. How did God address Moses' doubts about his abilities in Exodus 4:10-12? What comfort did Jesus offer His disciples in Luke 12:11-12?
4. Of what importance is teaching our children about God, according to Psalm 7:4-7? What is our purpose in passing on these truths?
5. Explain Titus 2:3-5. What is the significance of this passage, and how can it be followed?
6. What biblical principles should guide our teaching?

Give It Some Thought

1. What lessons can we take from Priscilla's encounter with Apollos in Acts 18:24-26?
2. What barriers impede your Bible study, and how can they be overcome?
3. What teachers have had the greatest impact on your spiritual development through the years? What made them special to you, and what lessons about teaching can you learn from them?
4. As Christian women, where can we plant seeds for the Lord by teaching others about Him?
5. We are urged to be both bold and gentle in teaching others about Christ (1 Peter 3:15). On their face, these terms seem contra-

dictory. How can we be bold without being abrasive, and gentle without avoiding the truth? What do these terms mean to you?

Give It a Try

1. Explore new ways to enhance your personal Bible study. Perhaps following a daily Bible reading schedule with a buddy, listening to the Bible on tape during a morning walk, or keeping a study journal would help your spiritual development.

2. Reread the opportunities to teach listed in this chapter. Do you see an area where you are needed, or can you think of another place where you could sow seeds for the Lord?

3. Invest in study materials that will help prepare you to teach. Study aids such as a good concordance, a sound commentary series, Bible software programs or religious periodicals might offer new wisdom for your study. Although the word of man should never replace the Word of God and should always be checked against the Bible, these resources might prove valuable tools for increasing knowledge and insight.

CHAPTER 10

ANSWERING WHEN GOD CALLS

"Be dressed in readiness, and keep your lamps alight. And be like men who are waiting for their master when he returns from the wedding feast, so that they may immediately open the door to him when he comes and knocks" (Luke 12:35-36).

Beads of perspiration dotted her forehead and trickled slowly down her back. Under the penetrating rays of the relentless summer sun, she had to squint to see the man standing at the city gate. Her stomach groaned with hunger, and her throat felt parched and swollen. She had not had a good meal in almost as many days as Zarephath had been without rain. She rose slowly to her feet, clutching a few brittle sticks to her breast. She felt light-headed and paused for a moment to steady herself.

As she made her way home, her steps were slow and deliberate. She did not look back toward the gate, but her mind did not move far from it. Dust swirled around her ankles as she walked across the hot, dry ground. The earth about her seemed to cry out for water, yet for another day the cloudless sky denied the land's unspoken pleas for rain. Like many of her townspeople, she prayed often for relief from this drought.

Quietly she entered her house, careful not to rouse her sleeping son. The sight of her little boy curled up in peaceful slumber brought a tender smile. His long eyelashes and curly mop of hair reminded her so much of her late husband. She stooped to kiss his cheek. His skin was still so soft and smooth, uncreased by worry and strain. His contentment gave her comfort. It had been difficult for her to provide for the two of them, but she simply trusted God each day and made the most of their meager provisions.

Eying their nearly empty bowl of flour, however, sadness gripped her heart as she realized that this day might be their last.

Through the window she could see the stranger still waiting. He had only asked her for a bread cake and water, but might as well have asked for gold and rubies. He promised that if she would serve him first, God would not let her go hungry. Looking from the stranger to her son, she felt conflicted. She had only enough flour and oil for one last meal for the two of them. She would not be able to forgive herself for taking their last morsels of food out of her son's mouth to feed a stranger, yet something about this man seemed so genuine. She had prayed fervently all morning that God would provide a way out for her. "Could this stranger really be a man of God?" she wondered. "Is he the answer to my prayers?" Her grumbling stomach yearned to be filled, yet she knew that her spirit must be stronger than her physical body.

After a few restless moments, she kindled a little fire and experience took over. As she had done so many times before, she dipped her hand into the bowl and scooped out a handful of flour. She poured some oil into the flour and patted the moist dough into a little cake. She placed the patty into the pan, where it cooked quickly. The aroma of the bread cake tempted her empty stomach, but she refused to give in to her hunger.

Instead, the widow turned and filled a jar with the water she had been saving for her last supper. When the bread was cool enough to handle, she took the water in one hand and the little cake in the other. As she walked to the city gate, she prayed with the faith of a woman who was spiritually filled. When at last she reached the stranger, she had no words. As she extended her hands to him, she smiled realizing that prayers are often answered in mysterious ways. "Sometimes, in order to accept the Lord's blessings," she mused, "we must open our hands and let go of all that we have."

The widow of Zarephath's story of faith is so moving and so inspiring. We meet her in 1 Kings 17. The prophet Elijah had been dwelling east of the Jordan River at the brook Cherith. The land was experiencing a serious drought, but ravens provided food for him each day. When at last the brook dried up, God commanded

Elijah in verse 9, "Arise, go to Zarephath, which belongs to Sidon, and stay there; behold, I have commanded a widow there to provide for you." At the city gate, he found a woman gathering sticks and asked her for water. As she was about to get it, he also asked for a piece of bread. Verse 12 tells us,

> But she said, "As the Lord your God lives, I have no bread, only a handful of flour in the bowl and a little oil in the jar; and behold, I am gathering a few sticks that I may go in and prepare for me and my son, that we may eat it and die."

Elijah assured her that the Lord would provide for her if she would oblige his request. The widow did as Elijah asked, and the Lord rewarded her faithfulness. She, Elijah and her household ate for many days and did not exhaust their supplies of flour and oil.

During what must have been a difficult, uncertain time in her life, this remarkable woman shared her food and her home with Elijah. Because of her generosity, the Lord provided for her physical needs. Her giving spirit was also rewarded when her son became so seriously ill that "there was no breath left in him" (v. 17). Elijah took the boy to the upper room and laid him on the bed. The prophet pleaded for the life of the widow's son. The Lord heard Elijah and restored the life of the child. This miracle convinced the widow that Elijah was truly a prophet.

Of all the women of the Bible we have studied thus far, the widow of Zarephath is among the most inspiring. Her courage and faithfulness amaze me. Under normal circumstances, giving a piece of bread and a drink of water to a stranger would be commendable, but probably not worth much recognition. Consider the extraordinary circumstances this woman was living in, however, and her choices take on much greater spiritual significance. Her actions during a time of tribulation showed great trust in God.

Periods of drought would have been challenging for all the townspeople of her day, but they would have been even more difficult to bear for a woman with a dependent child and no provider. She probably spent much time on her knees pleading for God's mercy, hopeful that her household would escape starvation. As emaciated and weary as this mother must have been, it must have been more difficult for her to see her child becoming malnourished. Can't you imagine how she must have stretched her feeble resources? At last, despite her frugality, their food was nearly gone. How heavy her heart must have been as she gathered sticks at the city gate, knowing that she and her son would share one final meal together before they would starve.

Finally, when her future looked the bleakest and death was imminent, the answer to this unnamed woman's prayers came in a most surprising form. She might have expected the Lord's provisions to come by way of a kinsman who would become her redeemer or perhaps in the form of steady rain that would nourish the earth and end the famine. Prayers are often answered in the most unexpected ways, however, as this woman learned. Instead of sending a hero to her door with heaping baskets of food, God put in her path a hungry man at the city gate. Elijah requested water and bread, and the prophet stipulated that she was to prepare his food before preparing her own. God required that she put the needs of a stranger first. She met this challenge with strength and faith. She offered Elijah food at the city gate, and she went beyond what was commanded and offered him shelter for the duration of the drought. Out of her extreme poverty, this brave woman gave for all it was worth, and great was her reward. Her household was spared from starvation, and later her son was brought back to life.

This woman learned the powerful lesson that in order to accept the Lord's blessings, we must sometimes first open our hands and let go of what we have. The widow who went out to gather sticks at the city gate faced an uncertain future; her life and that of her son were at stake. Of all people, certainly she appeared least equipped to feed a stranger. She was willing to let go of her little bit of food, though, and in return the Lord rewarded her sacrifice with abundance. When we are willing to give our meager resources to the Lord, He will heap blessings on us. The challenge comes in trusting the Lord to provide.

This widow stands out from some of the other women we have studied because she gave to meet an urgent need. In other words, she answered when God called. Her example contrasts Lydia, Dorcas and Priscilla, for example, who seem to have ministered continually in one way or another. The grace of giving these three women displayed in offering hospitality, talent and teaching, respectively, would have been practiced repeatedly. Scripture does not indicate, however, that the widow of Zarephath had an ongoing ministry providing food and shelter for prophets or even an exceptional gift for hospitality. Her only preparation to serve in this unexpected way was her faith. She simply obeyed God when He asked her to give. Like this faithful widow, we can learn to seize opportunities to give when the Lord calls.

Called to Give

Jesus urged His disciples in Luke 12:35-36,

> Be dressed in readiness, and keep your lamps alight. And be like men who are waiting for their master when he returns from the wedding feast, so that they may immediately open the door to him when he comes and knocks.

Of course, we all want to be prepared for our Savior's ultimate, triumphal return. However, spiritual readiness is more than being prepared to meet the Lord at the end of our lives. Being ready to respond to Christ means keeping our eyes open to the urgent needs around us. If we want to be ready to meet the Lord when He comes, we must strive to answer when He calls day by day.

As Christians, we must strive daily to bear fruit in the kingdom of God. This fruit comes as a result of faithful service in the church and in the lives of the people around us. First John 3:17-18 points out that our love for God is demonstrated through our propensity to serve:

> But whoever has the world's goods, and beholds his brother in need and closes his heart against him, how does the love of God abide in him? Little children, let us not love with word or with tongue, but in deed and truth.

When needs arise in our congregations and communities, the world will see the love of God through the actions we take.

The Lord might knock on your door at home through a friend who is experiencing a family crisis or a sick child who needs extra attention. At church, the Lord might call through news of a death in a member's family, announcements made for several weeks pleading for a cradle roll teacher, or urgent news of a missionary experiencing financial hardship. If we are spiritually alert, we will be prepared to respond when we are needed.

Paul understood keenly the important role Christians play in caring for each other. He urged in Titus 3:14, "And let our people also learn to engage in good deeds to meet pressing needs, that they may not be unfruitful." This apostle and missionary was blessed on numerous occasions by the generosity of his brothers and sisters in Christ. In his missionary journeys, he sometimes depended on the kindness of the saints for food, clothing and shelter. He advised Timothy in 1 Timothy 6:18-19,

> Instruct them to do good, to be rich in good works, to be generous and ready to share, storing up for themselves the treasure of a good foundation for the future, so that they may take hold of that which is life indeed.

Paul could not have had as great an impact in spreading the gospel without his fellow Christians keeping their eyes open to urgent needs and readily giving when aid was required. In fact, the church could not have grown as it did in its early days without Christians who were eager to minister. The same is true for the church of our Lord today.

Sacrifice and the Second Mile

When faced with an urgent need, our reflex should be to give without worrying whether our own needs will be met. This is difficult to do, but our faith in God will be strengthened as we learn to serve others freely. The widow of Zarephath, who had nothing to spare, gave without taking care of her own needs first. She risked starvation for herself and her household by feeding Elijah. Because of her willingness to serve him first, she learned that the Lord rewards sacrifice with abundance. The nature of our Lord is still the same today. Amazingly, the more we respond to those in need, the more we will find that our own needs will be met. If God asks us to serve, He will supply us the means to give and will reward our faithfulness.

When God calls, we have the responsibility to do what is required. However, like the widow, we should strive to go beyond the call of duty in our efforts to serve. Jesus urged in Matthew 5:41, "And who-ever shall force you to go one mile, go with him two." In Jesus' day citizens were required by law to carry the load of a Roman soldier for one mile if asked. Jesus' followers would have been familiar with this command, and probably most had been asked to do so from time to time. Consider how physically challenging and inconvenient this task could have been. Going the first mile with a good attitude was probably difficult at times, so choosing to go an extra mile would have been a new and surprising concept for Jesus' audience. The second mile of service truly would have been an unexpected sac-rifice. The first mile was the mile of duty, and the second was the mile of love. This bears out today. Meeting an urgent need may be a reflexive action borne out of necessity, but continuing to serve beyond filling an immediate need comes because of love.

This point is well demonstrated in the story of the widow of Zarephath. As the Lord required, she gave Elijah the bread and wa-ter he requested at the city gate. When she gave him his first morsels of food, she was obligated by duty. He was a stranger to her at that point, someone she knew nothing about. Her service in their first encounter revealed more about her trust in God than her concern for the person Elijah. In her second-mile service, however, she opened her home to Elijah and shared her food with him for the duration of the drought. How different it must have been to share her resources with him after he had been a guest in her home. In the months that he visited with her, their growing friendship would have compelled her to share her food and resources with him. Her compassion for him as an individual would have made going the second mile a matter of choice rather than compulsion.

The same proves true for us today. Although sometimes the bur-dens of the first mile may seem heavy, joy and comradery will ease the load of the second mile. The more we know and care for peo-ple, the easier it will be for us to open our eyes to their worries, an-ticipate their needs, and offer our support. Sacrifices made in the second mile of service might actually be greater than those re-quired in the first, but compassion and understanding will allow us to do whatever is needed.

Ultimately, we can rest assured that no matter what mile of ser-vice we find ourselves in, we will never have to walk alone. Our

Lord promises to be a steady and faithful companion. He invites us in Matthew 11:28-30,

> Come to Me, all who are weary and heavy-laden, and I will give you rest. Take My yoke upon you, and learn from Me, for I am gentle and humble in heart; and you shall find rest for your souls. For My yoke is easy, and My load is light.

As we go through life meeting needs of the people we meet, our Lord will be right beside us. He promises that we will not have to bear our burdens alone. He will give us the strength, compassion and stamina we need to serve.

Women Who Are Willing

Through *Christian Woman* magazine, I have had opportunity to interview some ordinary women who minister in extraordinary ways. These remarkable women share several characteristics. First, their eyes are open to opportunities to share God's love. Second, they accept challenges to give and trust the Lord to provide. And finally, ultimately they feel more blessed than those they have served. I introduce three of these special ladies to you now.

• *Child of the Kings.* Donna King could never have imagined how much her life would change as a result of an announcement made at the Greenwood Park Church of Christ in Bowling Green, Ky., where her husband then served as youth minister. A vanload of children flown into the United States from Guatemala would be arriving soon in Bowling Green to receive medical treatment, and host families were needed to house the children during their tenure. "I immediately felt that that was something the Lord wanted me to do," Donna told me from her Nashville, Tenn., home.

After talking with her husband, Russ, and their three daughters, the Kings made a prayerful decision to become a host family. Within a few days, 9-year-old Claudia Susanna Vasquez-Hernandez found in the Kings her home away from home. Susi had contracted polio when she was 11 months old, and severe scoliosis resulted. The Kings served as Susi's host family for nine months during preparations for spinal lateral fusion, surgery and recovery. Then, four years later, Susi returned to the United States for a second spinal lateral fusion to correct the bottom half of her spine. This stay lasted more than a year. Susi's stay brought many challenges, but Donna remained positive throughout. "Even in the hard times, the Lord gives you strength to do what you have to do," she said.

Donna said she and her daughters grew spiritually because of their experiences with Susi. "This has been one of the best ways to teach them to serve," she shared during our interview. "They have had to take on extra responsibilities, and we have all had to do things we didn't think we could do." Susi touched each family member in a special way, and with each visit it was difficult to contemplate her return to Guatemala. After spending time in Donna's loving home, I found that what had first sounded like a mission effort was really a family. And Susi was no ordinary foster child; she was a child of the Kings.

• *The Courage to Convert.* Several years ago, I began a friendship with an amazing lady named Mary Mott, then of Arlington, Va. At 70, Mary was not one to let an opportunity to talk about the gospel pass. Whether on the subway, on the street, or even on the phone with a telemarketer, she took advantage of often missed, everyday opportunities to share her faith.

Mary also saw potential in people many other Christians would disregard as unlovable, unteachable, unapproachable and unforgivable. She shocked friends and family when she decided to reach out to cannibal and convicted killer Jeffrey Dahmer after seeing a TV interview with Dahmer and his father.

"I thought, these two people are void … . They're reaching for something, and they don't know what it is," she explained. Mary quickly sent a letter, a Bible and correspondence courses "with a stamp and a prayer." When she received a response a few weeks later, she was so excited she left the rest of her mail with the postman. Dahmer's completed correspondence courses indicated that he wanted to be baptized, so Mary contacted a minister near Portage, Wis., where he was imprisoned.

Even after Dahmer's prison beating and death, many people still expressed doubts that a man who had committed such heinous acts of violence could change, but Mary's response was that salvation is in the hands of God. She pointed out the similarity between Dahmer and Paul. No doubt, she said, Paul sometimes worshiped side by side with Christians whose parents, children or friends he had persecuted or killed. "I'm sure Paul had trouble convincing Christians that he had changed and that he didn't want to persecute them, but we don't question his sincerity today," Mott said. "I don't agree with anything Jeff did, but I do agree that God can forgive anything, no matter how terrible."

• *Standing for the Lord.* Missy Jenkins of Paducah, Ky., credits God, her family and her friends with helping her through the years since a shooting spree at Paducah's Heath High School claimed the lives of several classmates and put her in a wheelchair. In a move that shocked many people and garnered national attention, soon after the tragic shooting Missy and her family gave shooter Michael Carneal a priceless gift: forgiveness. And despite grueling physical therapy and other challenges, Missy has not wavered from her positive outlook.

The bullet that entered her back couldn't touch her faith, and she says her experiences since the shooting have helped her grow spiritually. "My faith in God hasn't changed," she told me as a high school senior. "It's been good." People across the country have remained interested in Missy's progress, and she has proven a positive role model for young and old. Traveling around the nation, she speaks to youth groups about her faith, school violence and being in a wheelchair.

As for her future, Missy sees great things ahead. A college freshman when we last talked, she said she plans a career working with disabled teens and foresees getting out of her wheelchair for good. "I think I'll walk again," she said. "I truly believe God will give me that chance."

Prepared to Answer

Answering God's call can be difficult. As in the story of the widow of Zarephath, He might come to our door in an unexpected way or at a time when we feel least equipped to serve. It can be easy to miss these opportunities, but with faith we can overcome these barriers to meeting urgent needs.

• *Closing Our Eyes to Opportunities to Serve.* This might happen because we become too caught up in our own lives. Life seems to move at a faster pace every day, but we should never let ourselves get so busy or self-involved that we cannot respond to the Lord. It takes focus and desire to listen for God's call. Perhaps sometimes we see needs, but neglect to do our part because we assume that other people will take care of it. "That's not my job," we reason. We can always find someone we feel bears more responsibility to serve, whether a preacher, teacher, elder, deacon or family member. All Christians, however, must work together in the body. Perhaps others will contribute, but wouldn't it be a blessing to people in need to see kindness overflowing from God's people?

• *"That's Not My Gift."* When asked to serve, we might quickly refuse because we feel inadequate to the task. "I wouldn't know what to say"; "I have no talent in that area"; or "I'm not good in those situations," we might say. Obedience to God, however, demands that we step outside our comfort zones. The Bible is filled with unwilling vessels that God was able to use for His purposes. Consider Moses, who didn't want to lead (Exodus 3); Jonah, who didn't want to teach (Jonah 1-4); and David, who was too small to kill a giant (1 Samuel 17). We serve the same God today, and we can do all things through Him who strengthens us (Philippians 4:13). When faced with an intimidating opportunity, prayerful consideration might lead us to stretch ourselves to serve in new ways.

• *Opportunity Catches Us Unprepared.* Our preparations for the arrival of the Bridegroom should include being prepared to respond to opportunities to serve Him now. Preparation doesn't guarantee opportunity, but being unprepared does guarantee that we won't seize opportunities when they come. Let us strive to keep our lights burning so that we will be ready to serve the Lord.

• *A "One and Done" Mentality.* As a "things to do" person, I get a charge out of having a list of tasks and crossing them off one by one. Although this strategy may serve us well for managing our households, we must be careful not to carry this attitude over into our spiritual lives. It can be tempting to mark people off our list of priorities after we have served them once. Many needs take time to fill, however, and we must be patient. When we serve other people, our focus should be on developing a relationship.

• *Satan Whispers, "That's a Good Idea ... But Why Don't You Wait?"* Procrastination can be the most effective barrier to our answering God's call to give. We may see a need, but doubt whether we should act right then. Maybe now is not a good time, we reason. Is there ever really a bad time, though, to know that we are loved? We must be sensitive in responding to those in need, of course, but we can't let fear keep us from acting at all. Perhaps we hesitate to lend a hand because we don't know how our efforts will be taken. "I don't know what they'll think of me," we worry. Perhaps we will catch the world off guard by our kindness, but that is how our Lord says it should be:

> You are the light of the world. A city set on a hill cannot be hidden. Nor do men light a lamp, and put it under the peck-measure, but on the lampstand; and it gives light to all who are in the house. Let your light shine before men in such a way that they may see your good works, and glorify your Father who is in heaven (Matthew 5:14-16).

Serving the Lord

Amazing things happen when we meet people's needs in a way that is pleasing to God. Those we serve glimpse the face of Jesus in us as they experience our compassion. The truth is before most people will ever read a Bible or enter a church building, they will look to the people who wear the name Christian. Our lives must be worthy of the One we serve. As Christ's ambassadors, we must strive to show the world His mercy and compassion. If we are able to serve people with love and faithfulness, people will be drawn to the Christ they see dwelling in us.

Likewise, as we grow to care about those we serve, we will come to see the face of Jesus in them. As we learn to care more deeply about the people around us, we will recognize their spiritual significance in God's eyes. This will allow us to look beyond their bad choices and troubled pasts to see people who are just like us – struggling souls in need of a Savior. As we grow in empathy and compassion, generosity will come easily and our Lord will be pleased and glorified.

For What It's Worth

Titus 3:14 urges, "And let our people also learn to engage in good deeds to meet pressing needs, that they may not be unfruitful."

Whenever God asks us to give, we can trust that He will supply the means to give. The widow of Zarephath responded to God's call by sharing her food and water with Elijah. She learned that when we open our hands and let go of what we have, the Lord heaps blessings upon us. She serves as an example for us today because of her willingness to sacrifice to meet urgent needs and to give beyond what was required. We, too, have opportunities to give when the Lord calls. Although these opportunities may be easy to overlook or may seem too difficult, Jesus promises to be with us. He will give us the strength, courage and compassion we need to help meet the needs of those around us. Ultimately, our good deeds will demonstrate the love of Christ, bringing honor and glory to our Lord.

Give an Answer

1. Recount the story of the widow of Zarephath, as told in 1 Kings 17.
2. Read Luke 12:35-36. Explain the dual application of this passage in context of our preparation to meet the Bridegroom.
3. What points can we take from 1 Timothy 6:18-19?
4. What kind of sacrifices does Jesus want His followers to make in His name (Matthew 5:41)? What does He promise in return (11:28-30)?
5. How many Bible characters can you cite who were able to serve God beyond their limited circumstances, abilities or expectations?
6. How does meeting the needs of other people impact our salvation, according to Matthew 25:34-36, 40?

Give It Some Thought

1. What spiritual lessons from the story of the widow of Zarephath touch you most?
2. Discuss the role of sacrifice in second-mile service. What are the rewards of going beyond the call of duty?
3. Have you ever relied on the kindness of another person during a crisis? How has this experience affected your ability to see and respond to the needs of other people in similar circumstances?

4. What factors can hinder us from meeting urgent needs, and how can they be overcome?

5. How do our good deeds show the face of Jesus?

Give It a Try

1. If you have a spare bedroom, fix it up as a cozy retreat and make it available to your congregation as a "prophets' room" for visiting preachers, stranded travelers, newcomers to the community, or anyone else who might need your hospitality.

2. Sing some songs that will encourage you to give when God calls, such as "A Beautiful Life," "Follow Me," "Jesus Calls Us," "My Task" or "Is Your Life a Channel of Blessing?"

3. This week choose one topic from a previous chapter – or a different topic for each day of the week – and challenge yourself to find opportunities to give in that way. Keep a record of the opportunities you see each day.

CHAPTER 11

WE BOW DOWN

"Come, let us worship and bow down; Let us kneel before the Lord our Maker. For He is our God, And we are the people of His pasture, and the sheep of His hand" (Psalm 95:6-7).

Kneeling on the temple floor, Anna was the picture of humble solitude. With head bowed, her crown of gray hair glistened like silver under a beam of light streaming through a nearby window. Deep in prayer, Anna did not notice the young family enter.

Once inside the temple, the new mother stopped briefly to reposition her baby's blanket. Her husband's expression was earnest as he wrapped his strong arm around her. In accordance with the Law of Moses, the couple had come to Jerusalem to present their infant son to the Lord and to offer a sacrifice on his behalf. As the young mother looked tenderly from her baby to his solemn father, the infant snuggled contentedly in her arms. His happy gurgles roused Anna, and she smiled at the sight before her. They looked like so many of the new families Anna had seen in her 84 years – beaming with pride over their new baby and full of hope for his future. Anna had seen countless scenes like this, yet the pleasure and promise of each new baby still filled her heart with joy.

Watching this family, however, Anna sensed something different, even special. From her vantage point on the temple floor, she watched with interest as the father gently guided his wife through the temple. As Anna's gaze settled on the child squirming in his mother's arms, words of the prophet Isaiah filled her mind:

> For a child will be born to us, a son will be given to us; and the government will rest on His shoulders; and His

name will be called Wonderful Counselor, Mighty God, Eternal Father, Prince of Peace.

"Praise God, who will not forget His people or leave them without help in time of trouble," she thought.

Since she was just a girl, Anna had hoped to see with her own eyes the Deliverer, the One God had promised. Looking at the infant's round, rosy face and tiny fingers, she smiled as she contemplated the wonder of God's plans. "Through a baby such as this one, so small and new, will come redemption," she thought. How amazing it would be to glimpse the majesty and perfection of God in such a tiny human form.

As she bowed her head again to pray, her mind returned to the words of Isaiah:

> And in that day you will say, "Give thanks to the LORD, call on His name. Make known His deeds among the peoples; make them remember that His name is exalted. Praise the LORD in song, for He has done excellent things; let this be known throughout the earth. Cry aloud and shout for joy, O inhabitant of Zion, for great in your midst is the Holy One of Israel."

It is in the second chapter of Luke that we meet 84-year-old prophetess Anna. Her story unfolds in verses 36-38, but reading the entire chapter gives a more complete picture. After the birth of Christ, we pick up the story of Mary and Joseph in verses 22-24. According to the Law of Moses, each firstborn male was to be presented in the temple. A pair of turtledoves or two young pigeons were to be sacrificed on his behalf. When Mary and Joseph took Jesus to the temple to fulfill the law, they encountered Simeon, a righteous and devout man to whom the Holy Spirit had revealed that "he would not see death before he had seen the Lord's Christ" (v. 26). Simeon took Jesus into his arms, blessed God and declared this child the One the Lord had promised. As Simeon prophesied to Jesus' bewildered parents about what was to come, Anna entered the picture.

> And there was a prophetess, Anna the daughter of Phanuel, of the tribe of Asher. She was advanced in

years, having lived with a husband seven years after her marriage, and then as a widow to the age of eighty-four. And she never left the temple, serving night and day with fastings and prayers. And at that very moment she came up and began giving thanks to God, and continued to speak of Him to all those who were looking for the redemption of Jerusalem (vv. 36-38).

Anna, who spent most of her life as a widow, gives us a beautiful example of a godly woman. When we meet her in Luke she is advanced in age, widowed and probably destitute, but these factors are not what set her apart as a great woman of God. In *All of the Women of the Bible*, Edith Deen says,

> More important is Anna's spirituality. The mention of her is so brief that little of her character can be given. But there is enough to liken her to a bright star that sweeps above the horizon and then suddenly dips down out of sight (Harper Collins, New York, 1955; p. 173).

Most of her lifetime was spent praying and fasting in the temple. Day after day she dedicated her life to worshiping the Lord. Her days of service stretched into months, the months into years, and the years into decades. Throughout, her worship was humble, expectant and joyful.

Because of her faithfulness, Anna was able to see the Christ child and prophesy about Him to other worshipers in the temple. After so many years spent in the temple, it must have been exhilarating when finally she glimpsed the Savior. I visualize Anna kneeling in prayer when across the temple she notices Simeon approaching Jesus and His parents. Her curiosity gives way to awe as she hears Simeon's pronouncement that Jesus is the Messiah. She rises quickly to her feet, her eyes filling with tears and her heart pounding. As she skips past people milling in the temple, she shares the exciting news with the astonished crowd. She feels nimble and light on her feet as she rushes to the young mother's side, rejoicing and thanking God.

Picturing Anna's reward for a lifetime of faithfulness is truly a beautiful image. After so many years of worshiping God in the temple, with her own eyes she finally saw the Christ child! At once she must have felt honored and humbled in His presence. In all her life, certainly nothing else would have compared to that moment.

Even if this devout woman had not seen God in the flesh, however, I think she still would have counted her life as blessed and fulfilling. The time she devoted to worshiping God in the temple would have enriched her life and spirit. Her godly focus, spiritual maturity and deep wisdom would have opened her eyes to the wonders of God in her daily life. Deen suggests,

> She was one of those who had time to enjoy all of God's beauties, such as the stars that lighted the sky at night, the dawn that broke in all its effulgent color over the Temple, and the setting sun as it dipped behind the tall spires shadowing the Temple's rugged stone walls (p. 174).

Through giving herself to God in worship, Anna was able to experience the blessing of a closer walk with her Father.

We, too, may experience the joys of communing with God. In fact, as Christians we can experience God in a more personal way than Anna did because the wall of separation between us and God was removed by Christ. Hebrews 10:19-22 encourages us,

> Since therefore, brethren, we have confidence to enter the holy place by the blood of Jesus, by a new and living way which He inaugurated for us through the veil, that is, His flesh, and since we have a great priest over the house of God, let us draw near with a sincere heart in full assurance of faith, having our hearts sprinkled clean from an evil conscience and our bodies washed with pure water.

Worshiping the Lord is our highest purpose and greatest task in this life. All of us have the means to give in this way. When we worship God, we allow ourselves to be a little more empty of ourselves and a little more full of God. Through worship we honor our Creator; we glimpse His majesty and power; we remember His sacrifice; we experience His love. Giving ourselves in worship is truly the best gift we can give our Father.

One on One with God

Our Lord desires for us to invite Him into our daily lives.

Ironically, the times when we feel least able to commune with God are the times we really need Him most. Christ gently pleads in Matthew 11:28-30,

> Come to Me, all who are weary and heavy-laden, and I will give you rest. Take My yoke upon you, and learn from Me, for I am gentle and humble in heart; and you shall find rest for your souls. For My yoke is easy, and My load is light.

During the busiest, most stressful times of our lives, our Father calls us to Him for calm and comfort. Our Lord promises in Matthew 28:20, "[L]o, I am with you always, even to the end of the age." He is always available to us through prayer and in His Word. This poem reminds me of God's strong, steady presence in our lives.

God's Day
by Melissa Lester

All night long I watched you sleep, snuggled in your
    bed.
I whispered softly My love for you and stroked your
    weary head.
I cradled you till the sun came up and you rose to
    meet the day.
I was eager to hear your waking thoughts, but you
    didn't take time to pray.
I knew what the day would hold for you – a new
    struggle in every task.
I knew that you would need My strength, but you
    didn't take time to ask.
With arms outstretched I walked with you as you
    faced a trying day.
I was ready and willing to carry your burdens, but
    you never glanced My way.
I showered you with blessings, and you accepted
    them all with glee.
I waited patiently for your thanks, but you had not a
    word for Me.
The day is coming to a close; the end is drawing
    near.

I walked beside you all the way, but you forgot that
   I was here.
You faced your troubles on your own, and now wor-
   ry fills your head.
How different your day could have been if you had
   leaned on Me instead.
Tomorrow is a new day, and I will walk with you
   again.
I hope that you will turn to Me – your Savior,
   Father, Friend.

Our relationship with God is much like any other significant relationship, in that communication will allow it to flourish. As in the
husband-wife relationship, we need times of brief, intermittent
interaction as well as times of deeper, more meaningful communion. My husband, Joe, usually calls me from work at least once
a day just to check in. During these brief phone calls, we share
events from our day and discuss little tasks that need to be done.
These conversations help us stay connected and up-to-date.
However, we also need time to connect on a deeper level – to open
our hearts, talk about our dreams, and share spiritual insights.
Both types of communication are vital to our relationship, and our
marriage would not be as strong if either type was neglected.

The need for communication in the marriage relationship can
be compared to our need to stay connected with God. Our hearts
will grow distant from our Lord if we neglect our need to com-
municate with Him. We need to devote significant periods of time
to God. We will grow spiritually through times of rich Bible study,
prayer and praise. These meaningful times allow us to open our
souls to God, sharpen our spiritual focus, and deepen our relationship with Him.

Our Lord knows we need time with Him. After John the Baptist
was beheaded, Jesus urged His weary, grieving apostles in Mark
6:31, "Come away by yourselves to a lonely place and rest a while."
Jesus invites us, too, to come away from our hurried lives to spend
one-on-one time with Him, and He promises to quiet and restore
our troubled souls. "Peace I leave with you; My peace I give to you;
not as the world gives, do I give to you. Let not your heart be troubled, nor let it be fearful," He soothes in John 14:27. Our devotional

times with the Lord will leave us spiritually refreshed and ready to meet the challenges of life.

Besides times of deep communion, we also need contact with the Lord as we go about our daily lives. Sometimes we look at our spiritual lives as somehow separate from our everyday lives, which distances us from God. This detrimental view robs us of the companionship we can experience with the Lord. He desires to walk with us, share our joys and carry our burdens, yet too often we go through our busy days without noticing or acknowledging His presence. James 5:13 urges, "Is anyone among you suffering? Let him pray. Is anyone cheerful? Let him sing praises." This verse conjures images of going to God throughout the day with our joys and sorrows, whether small or significant. This continual contact will help us stay close to Him. Maintaining a dialog with the Lord urges us to react spiritually to the events of the day, viewing our lives through a Christ-centered perspective.

Our Lord understands the challenges we face. He longs for us to turn to Him in good times and bad. As we strive to walk closer to Him each day, we will find ourselves transformed by the renewal of our minds, hearts and spirits. Hebrews 4:15-16 reminds us,

> For we do not have a high priest who cannot sympathize with our weaknesses, but one who has been tempted in all things as we are, yet without sin. Let us therefore draw near with confidence to the throne of grace, that we may receive mercy and may find grace to help in time of need.

Devoting time to God requires our diligence, but the peace and joy we will experience will make it well worth the effort.

Where Two or Three Are Gathered

Before Joe and I married, someone shared with us a poignant analogy that marriage is like a triangle between husband, wife and God. As both spouses draw closer to God, they will also move closer to each other.

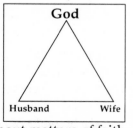

We have found this analogy to be true and believe that it bears out for other relationships, as well. Too often we feel inhibited talking about matters of faith outside the church building, but bringing God into any relationship will give it new depth and dimension. With freedom to talk about Bible passages, share spiritual struggles and marvel at the power of God in our lives, we move beyond relationships based solely on trivial or superficial matters. Instead we relate to each other on a spiritual level, offering support and encouragement as we strive to live in accordance with the Lord's will. We can be assured that any relationship with God in it will grow.

Keeping a spiritual focus will help keep God at the center of family life. Relationships between husband and wife, parent and child, or brother and sister will be strengthened when we relate to each other as children of God. A spiritual outlook will also help us take advantage of teachable moments. Time spent together in the beauty of nature will allow us to marvel at God's creation; thankfulness to God will characterize family celebrations; and difficult times will be approached from a spiritual perspective. With patterns of open communication, spouses can discuss matters of faith and children will feel free to ask questions. Time spent together in prayer, Bible study and singing will draw family members closer to God and to each other.

Relationships with our brothers and sisters in Christ are also strengthened when we keep them Christ-centered. With God at the heart of these relationships, we may experience the love of Christ on a very tangible level. "For where two or three have gathered together in My name, there I am in their midst," Christ promises in Matthew 18:20. As fellow Christians, we can nourish each other's faith by striving to fulfill Romans 12:10-13:

> Be devoted to one another in brotherly love; give preference to one another in honor; not lagging behind in diligence, fervent in spirit, serving the Lord; rejoicing in hope, persevering in tribulation, devoted to prayer, contributing to the needs of the saints, practicing hospitality.

The level of fellowship described here will take time and trust to develop. Only through time spent together one-on-one, away from the church building, will our relationships grow beyond a superficial level. At home, with our masks off and our defenses down, we will begin to relate to each other on a much more spiritually intimate level. In order to experience the friendship and support of our fellow Christians, we must be willing to reach out to each other with open hearts.

In our pursuit of holiness, we need the love and support of our brothers and sisters in Christ. Prayer plays an important role in these relationships, as James 5:13-20 suggests. Burdens of sickness, grief and worry are easier to bear when shared with members of God's family. Verses 14-15 instruct,

> Is anyone among you sick? Let him call for the elders of the church, and let them pray over him, anointing him with oil in the name of the Lord; and the prayer offered in faith will restore the one who is sick, and the Lord will raise him up, and if he has committed sins, they will be forgiven him.

God will hear and heed our prayers of faith on behalf of our brothers and sisters in Christ. Through confessing our struggles and offering counsel, we will be able to help each other stay on the right path. Verse 16 commands, "Therefore, confess your sins to one another, and pray for one another, so that you may be healed. The effective prayer of a righteous man can accomplish much."

Opening our hearts to each other about struggles and doubts will allow us to understand, strengthen and encourage each other. When fellow Christians struggle with illness, grief or sin, instead of just telling them we will pray for them, we can pray with them right then in their moment of struggle. Approaching the throne of God together to ask for His care, comfort or courage will bring unequaled, indescribable peace. As Christians walking together on the path of righteousness, we can spur each other on to greater faithfulness and service to God. Verses 19-20 counsel,

> My brethren, if any among you strays from the truth, and one turns him back, let him know that he who turns a sinner from the error of his way will save his soul from death, and will cover a multitude of sins.

As prayerful, compassionate Christians, our loads will be lighter and our paths will be brighter when we journey together.

The Body United

What a blessing it is to be a part of God's family, the church. Colossians 1:16-20 reminds us that the church was divinely planned, sacrificially bought and eternally sanctified by our Lord. The church was not an afterthought or an alternative idea. Called in Scripture Christ's body (Romans 12:5), His bride (Revelation 19:7), and His kingdom (Hebrews 12:28), the church was lovingly preordained. Indeed, Christ loves the church so much that Ephesians 5:25-27 urges husbands to follow His example.

The church is vital to our spiritual development. As a body of believers, we can spur each other on to greater spiritual heights than we could ever aspire to on our own. An important way we encourage this development is through coming together for worship. Praying together allows us to experience the peace of knowing that our Father is in control (Mark 11:24). Singing together praises of adoration fills us with joy and reminds us of the hope Christ offers us (Hebrews 2:11-12). Studying God's Word together and hearing the Gospel proclaimed allows for a deeper understanding of passages that might be overlooked or misinterpreted (2 Timothy 4:1-5). Confessing sins and struggles allows opportunities for encouragement and nourishment of the faith (James 5:16). Partaking of the Lord's Supper allows us to reflect on the sacrifice and supremacy of Christ (1 Corinthians 11:23-26; Acts 20:7). Our Father is pleased when we worship Him as He has commanded.

Truly, hours shared in corporate worship are the most important hours we spend each week. We must not allow ourselves to become lax or negligent in our commitment to worshiping together. Hebrews 10:23-25 urges,

> Let us hold fast the confession of our hope without wavering, for He who promised is faithful; and let us consider how to stimulate one another to love and good deeds, not forsaking our own assembling together ... but encouraging one another; and all the more, as you see the day drawing near.

Scripture commands our faithfulness in gathering as a body to worship. Although church attendance is not our only duty as Christians, it certainly is one indicator of our level of commitment to Christ. Hours dedicated to worshiping God with the saints can lay a good foundation for a life of godly service in His kingdom.

Our attitude toward worship is important. Instead of groaning that we have to go to worship services, we should rejoice that we get to go to worship. If we approach opportunities to gather for worship with joyful anticipation, our good attitudes will help nurture our children's love for worship. A friend shared with me how as a young girl her parents passed on an attitude of reverence for worship. "There was no arguing on Sunday mornings because you were going to worship," she said. Carole has fond memories of her father sitting in the recliner singing hymns on Sunday mornings. "He taught me that you have to prepare for worship. You don't just hit the building cold ready to worship God."

For What It's Worth

Anna devoted her life to worshiping God. We, too, should keep the Lord at the center of our lives. He invites us to cultivate personal relationships with Him. Through Bible study, prayer and praise, we sharpen our spiritual focus and renew our minds. Beyond this, bringing God into our relationships with other people will give these relationships new depth and dimension. With freedom to talk about Bible passages, share spiritual struggles and marvel at the power of God in our lives, we may spur each other on to greater service in the kingdom. We also have the privilege of coming together as a church family. Through time spent in corporate worship, we honor God and fortify our faith. When we worship God, we become a little more empty of ourselves and a little more full of God. This is the best gift we can give our Father.

Give an Answer

1. What do we know about the prophetess Anna from Luke 2?
2. Read Romans 12:2 and John 14:27. How does spending time alone with the Lord bring renewal and peace?
3. Discuss the importance of prayer in our relationships with other Christians according to James 5:13-20.
4. John 4:24 says, "God is spirit, and those who worship Him must worship in _____ and _____." Define those two terms.

5. What elements of corporate worship do we find described in the New Testament?

6. Our interaction with God, from our most private moments to our assemblies for corporate worship should be characterized by praise. What advice does Paul give us in Philippians 4:8 in regard to glorifying God even in the midst of trials and tribulation?

Give It Some Thought

1. What blessings do you think Anna experienced as a result of the years she devoted to worshiping God, and what can we learn from her today?

2. What two kinds of communication do we need in our personal relationships with God? Why are both types important?

3. Think of some ways to keep God at the center of family life.

4. Read Romans 12:10-13. Can you think of sisters in Christ who exemplify this passage? Do you demonstrate the level of compassionate commitment described?

5. Some people perceive a lack of joy in our congregational worship. Why do you think this is? How can we keep our worship from becoming stale or ritualistic without straying from New Testament patterns?

Give It a Try

1. For a praise-filled, joyful personal Bible study, read the book of Psalms.

2. Invite the youth of your congregation into your home for a devotional. You will find yourself encouraged by your interaction with teenagers, surprised by their spiritual insights, energized by their enthusiasm for the Lord, and uplifted by their heartfelt songs of praise.

3. Encourage your family to prepare for corporate worship by studying Bible class materials ahead of time, singing hymns and praying that your worship will be focused and pleasing to God.

CHAPTER 12

ALL I HAVE TO GIVE

"And you shall love the Lord your God with all your heart and with all your soul and with all your might" (Deuteronomy 6:5).

A s she and Joseph left the temple, Mary was quiet, contemplative. Still wide-eyed from the scene she had just witnessed, she looked slowly from Joseph to the infant snuggling in her arms. Baby Jesus yawned sleepily, unfazed by the commotion that had just taken place inside. He closed His eyes against the brightness of the sun, and Mary adjusted the blanket to shade His face. Within moments, He was asleep.

Like many other Jews of their day, Mary and Joseph had traveled to Jerusalem to make a sacrifice on behalf of their firstborn Son. As it was written in the Law of Moses, "Every first-born male that opens the womb shall be called holy to the Lord." In their pilgrimage to the temple, Mary felt reverent as she considered that she and her husband were following in the footsteps of the many families who had gone before them.

Once inside the temple, however, Mary was reminded once again that theirs was no ordinary journey into parenthood. When she and Joseph entered the temple, a man of God took Jesus into his arms. With great emotion, the man proclaimed the Baby to be the One God had promised. A prophetess also joined them, rejoicing and thanking God.

Now on their journey back to Galilee, at last Mary found herself alone with her thoughts. An introspective, sensitive young woman by nature, she had always tucked away experiences, pondering them in her heart. Especially during the last year, many times she had retreated to a private place to consider God's mighty works. Often she found she could not articulate her feelings even to Joseph; only with the Lord could she truly bare her soul. In moments of solitude, she would ponder His unfolding plans.

Looking at the sweet, perfect baby she now cradled, Mary marveled at her blessings. As she and Joseph traveled, she reflected on how God's hand had led her safely to this point. What a journey this had been! She could still remember the angel's stunning announcement that she, a virgin, would bear the Son of God. And since the angel, others had echoed his good tidings. Dear Elizabeth rejoiced even before Mary could share her good fortune. "Blessed among women are you, and blessed is the fruit of your womb!" she had exclaimed.

God had also sent shepherds to Bethlehem to celebrate Jesus' birth. Awed in His presence, the wondering shepherds had related the praises of the heavenly host. And what an amazing experience His birth had been … .

A hungry cry brought Mary back to the present. As Jesus stirred, Mary stroked His little face and kissed His soft cheeks. As she prepared to nurse Him, she looked deep into His eyes. "Oh, my little Son, do you know already that You will change the world?" she mused. "Already you have changed mine."

Mary turned her gaze heavenward for a moment, an unspoken prayer on her heart. As she looked again at the baby snuggling in her arms, a slight smile crept across His face. His little smile lit up His mother's face and brought a tear of joy as it penetrated her heart – a treasure to tuck away and cherish forever.

Truly, our study of biblical women who exemplify giving would be incomplete if we neglected to include the mother of our Lord. More than any other woman in Scripture, Mary epitomizes giving it all. God chose her from among all the women who have ever lived to be the mother, guardian and teacher of His Son during His earthly life. What an amazing woman she must have been to be chosen for such a task. God must have seen in her a compassionate, faithful servant – someone with whom He could entrust the care of His beloved Son. Her commitment to God carried her from the angel's announcement of the virgin birth to Jesus' earthly ministry, to His death on the cross, and finally, to His triumphal resurrection and ascension.

The Virgin Mary

Mary's story begins in the first chapter of Luke. Verses 26-27 tell us that an angel of the Lord appeared to Mary, a young virgin in Nazareth pledged to marry a man named Joseph. Gabriel shared with her the exciting, life-altering news that she had been chosen to be the mother of the Messiah. Mary's immediate response was humble and obedient: "Behold, the bondslave of the Lord; be it done to me according to your word" (v. 38). Her immediate willingness to serve God dramatically altered the course she probably had set for her life. In one moment, her life changed forever. In choosing to obey, she risked her future marriage, her family's favor and her reputation in the community. Yet Mary seemed never to count the costs of following God. In fact, Scripture does not indicate that she ever viewed Gabriel's news solely in terms of how it would affect her life. Instead, Mary joyfully assumed her role in God's plan with a spirit of humility and thankfulness.

Mary immediately went to the home of her relatives Zecharias and Elizabeth, who were expecting their first child. At the sound of Mary's voice, the baby in Elizabeth's womb leapt and Elizabeth was filled with the Holy Spirit. She praised Mary's faith and obedience in accepting God's call for her life. Mary's response in verses 46-55 reveals that rather than focusing on herself and how the prophesied events would impact her life, she viewed God's plans with a much broader perspective.

Mary spent the first trimester of her pregnancy with Zecharias and Elizabeth. I have often thought about how tenderly God cared for Mary during that time. How comforting it must have been for Mary to spend those first difficult months of pregnancy with Elizabeth. For many women, the early months of pregnancy are characterized by nausea, fatigue and fluctuating emotions. Add to that the unique circumstances of Mary's conception, and she could have felt hopelessly alone. But dear Elizabeth knew even before

Mary could tell her that she was carrying the Son of God. How relieved and encouraged Mary must have felt to hear Elizabeth's excitement. Certainly, Elizabeth's compassion and empathy must have given Mary tremendous strength. What a bond those two women of God must have had.

God also provided for Mary in giving her a faithful, understanding husband. The first chapter of Matthew gives the account of Jesus' conception from Joseph's perspective. This sensitive, godly man was surprised to learn that his bride was pregnant. Verse 19 tells us that Joseph, "not wanting to disgrace her, desired to put her away secretly." However, as he considered his options, an angel of the Lord told him in a dream,

> Joseph, son of David, do not be afraid to take Mary as your wife; for that which has been conceived in her is of the Holy Spirit. And she will bear a Son; and you shall call His name Jesus, for it is He who will save His people from their sins (vv. 20-21).

Joseph took Mary as his wife and patiently kept her a virgin until after she gave birth to Jesus.

Unto Us a Son Is Given

Luke 2 tells us about the birth of Jesus. Joseph took Mary to Bethlehem to register for the census. While in Bethlehem, Mary went into labor. Joseph was unable to find a comfortable place for his wife to give birth, so the King of kings and Lord of lords made His way into the world in the humblest of circumstances: "And she gave birth to her first-born son; and she wrapped Him in cloths, and laid Him in a manger, because there was no room for them in the inn" (v. 7). What images this story evokes. The Gospel accounts of the virgin birth have inspired countless works of art and music over the centuries. Beloved hymns like "Away in a Manger," "O, Little Town of Bethlehem" and "Silent Night" remind us of the wonder and significance of that starry night so long ago.

While Mary and Joseph rested in their makeshift hospital, shepherds came to Bethlehem to find baby Jesus lying in the manger. The shepherds brought with them awesome accounts of the angelic announcement of Jesus' birth.

Luke 2:18-19 says, "And all who heard it wondered at the things which were told them by the shepherds. But Mary treasured up all these things, pondering them in her heart." Here we are given a glimpse into Mary's reflective nature. In verse 51, we are told again that she "treasured all these things in her heart." She seems to have been a private, thoughtful and perhaps introverted woman. Her contemplative nature probably served her well in her role as the mother of Jesus, for many of the fantastic events she witnessed were probably best tucked away to be studied and understood later.

A trip to the temple to offer a sacrifice on Jesus' behalf yielded more prophecies about what was to come for this young mother. We examined the events that took place in the temple from Anna's perspective in our last chapter, but it is also interesting to approach this occasion from Mary's perspective. When Mary and Joseph took their infant Son to the temple, devout Simeon took Jesus into His arms and proclaimed Him the Messiah. Luke 2:33 tells us that "His father and mother were amazed at the things which were being said about Him." Simeon blessed Mary and Joseph and told Mary,

> Behold, this Child is appointed for the fall and rise of many in Israel, and for a sign to be opposed – and a sword will pierce even your own soul – to the end that thoughts from many hearts may be revealed (vv. 34-35).

How Mary must have mulled over Simeon's message in the years to come.

Sweet Mother Mary

Returning to Matthew, we learn more about Jesus' early days. Chapter 2 begins,

> Now after Jesus was born in Bethlehem of Judea in the days of Herod the king, behold, magi from the east arrived in Jerusalem, saying, "Where is He who has been born King of the Jews? For we saw His star in the east, and have come to worship Him" (vv. 1-2).

Evil Herod was afraid that a successor would arise to take his throne from him one day, so he began plotting to keep his kingdom from being overthrown. He learned from the chief priests and scribes that the Christ was to be born in Bethlehem. Then he ascertained from the wise men when the star had appeared. Herod then sent the magi to Bethlehem, saying, "Go and make careful search for the Child; and when you have found Him, report to me, that I too may come and worship Him" (v. 8).

The magi followed the star they had seen in the east, which led them to Jesus. Verse 11 recounts their visit with the Christ child:

> And they came into the house and saw the Child with Mary His mother; and they fell down and worshiped Him; and opening their treasures they presented to Him gifts of gold and frankincense and myrrh.

Warned by God in a dream not to return to Herod, the wise men left Jesus and returned home by another route. Herod was enraged when the magi did not return to him, and he ordered that all male children ages 2 and under in Bethlehem and surrounding areas be killed. This horrible time fulfilled prophecies of Jeremiah:

> A voice was heard in Ramah, weeping and great mourning, Rachel weeping for her children; and she refused to be comforted, because they were no more (Matthew 2:18).

Through God's providence, Jesus' life was spared. After the wise men left their home, an angel of the Lord urged Joseph in a dream to flee with Mary and Jesus to Egypt. Joseph was quick to respond:

> And he arose and took the Child and His mother by night, and departed for Egypt; and was there until the death of Herod, that what was spoken by the Lord through the prophet might be fulfilled, saying, "Out of Egypt did I call My Son" (vv. 14-15).

Again an angel appeared to Joseph in a dream when it was safe to return to the land of Israel. The family returned to Israel, but Joseph feared that Judea would not provide a safe haven for Mary and Jesus. God warned him to depart for the region of Galilee, so Joseph took the family to Nazareth. How relieved Mary and Joseph must have been when at last they were able to settle into a home.

In Nazareth, Mary assumed normal duties as a wife and mother. Scripture does not give us many details of Jesus' growing up, except to tell us, "And the Child continued to grow and become strong, increasing in wisdom; and the grace of God was upon Him" (Luke 2:40). Mary and Jesus probably spent many precious hours together during His boyhood years, studying God's Word and sharing household duties.

Each year Mary and Joseph traveled to Jerusalem for the Passover. When Jesus was 12, He stayed behind in Jerusalem after His parents began their journey home. Unaware that He was not in the caravan, Mary and Joseph traveled for a day before realizing that young Jesus was not with any of their friends or relatives. The worried parents returned to Jerusalem to look for their Son. What an anguished three days Mary and Joseph must have spent before they finally found Jesus in the temple, listening to and questioning the teachers. Scripture tells us,

> His mother said to Him, "Son, why have You treated us this way? Behold, your father and I have been anxiously looking for You." And He said to them, "Why is it that you were looking for me? Did you not know that I had to be in My Father's house?" (Luke 2:48-49).

Mary and Joseph, perplexed by their Son's response, took Jesus home to Nazareth. Perhaps as Mary thought about Jesus' actions and His words to her in the temple, she glimpsed what was to come in His earthly ministry. This incident must have reminded her that Jesus had come to earth to do His heavenly Father's work.

Back in Nazareth, life once again achieved a semblance of normalcy. Jesus was a faithful, respectful Son. Verses 51-52 say,

> He continued in subjection to them; and His mother treasured all these things in her heart. And Jesus kept increasing in wisdom and stature, and in favor with God and men.

Mary must have beamed with pride as she watched Jesus grow and mature, ever mindful that like Hannah, she was preparing her Son for greater service.

This greater service began for Jesus when He was about 30 years old. It is interesting to note that there is no mention of Joseph from this point on in Scripture. He probably died before Jesus' ministry began, but we are not told. Later on, Jesus asked John to care for His mother, so it would appear that Mary was widowed at some point.

Mother of the King

As He began His Father's work, Mary was still a strong presence in the life of Jesus. After His baptism by John the Baptist, Jesus accompanied His mother and His disciples to a wedding feast in Cana of Galilee. When Mary realized that the hosts had run out of wine, she reported the shortage to Jesus. Jesus answered, "Woman, what do I have to do with you? My hour has not yet come" (John 2:4). However, Mary instructed the servants to do whatever Jesus said, and He proceeded to turn water to wine. This first miracle impressed the wedding guests and opened the eyes of Jesus' followers. Verse 11 says, "This beginning of His signs Jesus did in Cana of Galilee, and manifested His glory, and His disciples believed in Him."

After the wedding, Mary accompanied Jesus and His disciples to Capernaum for a few days. We do not know how much time Mary spent with Jesus in the three years that followed. Reading about the events of Jesus' ministry – from His turning over the tables of the money changers in the temple (vv. 14-16), to His preaching and healing throughout Israel (Matthew 4:23-25) – it is interesting to wonder how much Mary witnessed. We know she supported Jesus throughout His ministry and was faithful to the end. Do you think she was sometimes amazed to see the signs and wonders Jesus performed? Perhaps she marveled when she heard Him teach, remembering the boy who once sat at her knee. As a mother, did she sometimes worry that He might suffer harm at the hands of His critics?

Mary's worst possible fears did come true when Jesus was arrested and sentenced to die by crucifixion. Ever faithful to her Son, Mary at last found herself at the foot of the cross. As His mother, she alone was with Him at both His birth and His death. With such joy she had welcomed Him into the world; how agonizing it must have been to let Him go. I wonder whether scenes treasured in her heart flashed before her at the foot of the cross. Did she remember the angel's announcement that she, a virgin, would give birth to the Son of God? As she watched her Son in agony, struggling between life and death, did Simeon's words of long ago, "and a sword will pierce even your own soul" (Luke 2:35), echo in her mind? As He cried, "I am thirsty" (John 19:28), did her heart break remembering the baby she had once nursed? Did her heart feel some sense of relief when at last His torture was ended and He had gone home?

Before returning to His heavenly home, Jesus made provisions for Mary's care:

> When Jesus therefore saw His mother, and the disciple whom He loved standing nearby, He said to His mother, "Woman, behold, your son!" Then He said to the disciple, "Behold, your mother!"' And from that hour the disciple took her into his own household (John 19:26-27).

In this passage, we see that Jesus deeply loved Mary. Henry Wadsworth Longfellow supposed,

> Even He that died for us upon the cross, in the last hour … was mindful of His Mother, as if to teach us that this holy love should be our last worldly thought, the last point of earth from which the soul should take its flight for heaven.

As Jesus endured indescribable pain and suffering on the cross, He knew that His mother agonized with Him. He wanted her to know that she would be protected and cared for.

Thankfully, Mary's journey as the mother of the Savior did not end with Jesus' crucifixion, for three days later He triumphed over the grave and rose again. Acts 1:3 tells us that He spent 40 days on earth, "speaking of the things concerning the kingdom of God." How His mother must have treasured those last days. To see Jesus alive again must have helped dim the painful, haunting images of His crucifixion. To be able to speak with Him and to see Him preaching and teaching again must have brought her such joy. Perhaps mother and Son spent a few private moments together before He was taken up into heaven again.

After Jesus' ascension from Mount Olivet, His disciples returned to Jerusalem, where they met in the upper room of the home where the apostles were staying. There they communed together: "These all with one mind were continually devoting themselves to prayer, along with the women, and Mary the mother of Jesus, and with His brothers" (Acts 1:14). Together they prayed and prepared themselves for what was to come.

Mary was probably still with the group when on the Day of Pentecost the Holy Spirit came upon the apostles and the church was established. Perhaps she was one of the faithful souls added to the church that day. What a lovely image it is to picture Mary's story culminating in her own baptism. How she must have thought of her Son and Savior at that moment, knowing that His kingdom had come. After our study of Mary and all that she experienced, how comforting it is to leave her in the safe haven of the brothers and sisters in Christ mentioned in Acts 2:46-47:

> And day by day continuing with one mind in the temple, and breaking bread from house to house, they were taking their meals together with gladness and sincerity of heart, praising God, and having favor with all the people. And the Lord was adding to their number day by day those who were being saved.

My Friend Mary

Mary truly epitomizes the selfless woman of God. She fulfilled Deuteronomy 6:5 with grace and humility: "And you shall love the Lord your God with all your heart and with all your soul and with all your might." Through her story of lifelong service, she sets a beautiful example of giving all we have to give.

Despite her humble spirit and unassuming nature, before I came to know her more intimately through Scripture, Mary was an intimidating character to me. In my heart of hearts, I wondered if I really could relate to her story or aspire to emulate her service to God. After all, how could any woman today ever hope to compare to this woman whom Scripture calls "favored one" and "blessed among women" (Luke 1:28, 42)?

It was not until this study began that I realized the most beautiful, poignant aspect of the story of Mary: She gave all that she had to give, not by achieving worldly status or accomplishing unbelievable feats, but by being a mother. Through this simple role, she forever changed the world. Although a miracle was performed in her, Mary did not perform miracles herself. Yet through assuming the role of mother – a role held by countless women before and since her time – Mary had a greater impact on the world for good than any other woman in Scripture. Truly, there is no ambassador for God with as much influence in the life of her child as a mother. Elisabeth Elliot echoes this sentiment:

> A mother is a chalice, the vessel without which no human being has ever been born. She is created to be a life-bearer, cooperating with her husband and with God in the making of a child. What a solemn responsibility. What an unspeakable privilege – a vessel divinely prepared for the Master's use.

Through their love and guidance, mothers have great power to lead their children to the Lord.

Looking beyond Mary's specific role as a mother, her story has broader application for all Christian women. The lesson for us today is to serve God eagerly, selflessly and humbly in whatever roles we find ourselves. Whether as mothers, daughters, sisters, wives, grandmothers, friends, students or professionals, we glorify God when we strive to serve Him from our unique spheres of influence. Like Mary, we honor our Lord when we fulfill the roles He gives us – however seemingly grand or small – with godly focus.

With this new perspective on Mary's service to God, we can find a new friend in her. Once a distant hero, I now see her as someone who can inspire me to give all of my heart, soul and might to the Lord. I have also come to see Mary in so many of the Christian women around me – women who serve God faithfully every day in their homes and congregations.

All of Heart, Soul and Might

Like Mary, we will please God when we give Him all of ourselves. If we are willing to sacrifice our will to God with humility and faith, our lives can become vessels through which other people will come to know His love. Scripture gives us guidance in how to serve Him with all of our hearts, souls and might. Ten qualities needed for godly service are listed here.

• *Desire.* "Whom have I in heaven but Thee? And besides Thee, I desire nothing on earth. My flesh and my heart may fail, But God is the strength of my heart and my portion forever" (Psalm 73:25-26). Desire is the first step toward giving ourselves to God.

He has blessed us so richly. Realizing His great love for us will inspire us to serve Him. With our hearts turned toward Him with love and thankfulness, we will seek to lead God-pleasing lives.

• *Direction.* "But seek first His kingdom and His righteousness; and all these things shall be added to you" (Matthew 6:33). Grounded in the Word of God and committed to prayer, serving God will become a priority that permeates all that we do. Keeping Him first will help direct our steps on the path of righteousness, so we may fulfill 2 Thessalonians 3:5: "And may the Lord direct your hearts into the love of God and into the steadfastness of Christ."

• *Duty.* "For we are His workmanship, created in Christ Jesus for good works, which God prepared beforehand, that we should walk in them" (Ephesians 2:10). Like Jesus, we must remember to be about our Father's business. Our eyes and ears should be open to opportunities to serve, and our hands and feet must be ready for action.

• *Devotion.* "For I am jealous for you with a godly jealousy; for I betrothed you to one husband, that to Christ I might present you as a pure virgin. But I am afraid, lest as the serpent deceived Eve by his craftiness, your minds should be led astray from the simplicity and purity of devotion to Christ" (2 Corinthians 11:2-3). Satan is always eager to shift our focus to things of the world. We must keep our eyes fixed on things above, always seeking to please our Lord.

• *Drive.* "And we know that God causes all things to work together for good to those who love God, to those who are called according to His purpose" (Romans 8:28). We must have passion for the Lord's work. All things do work together for those who love God, but sometimes the good result at the journey's end looms too far ahead for our eyes to see. With trust in the Lord and enthusiasm for His cause, we will be able to maintain the focus and stamina needed for running the Christian race.

• *Discipline.* "All discipline for the moment seems not to be joyful, but sorrowful; yet to those who have been trained by it, afterwards it yields the peaceful fruit of righteousness" (Hebrews 12:11). We must strive to live honorable, disciplined lives so we will not be tempted to stray from God's path. Reading the Bible, praying and cultivating relationships with fellow Christians will help us live fully and faithfully in a way that pleases and honors our Father.

• *Diligence.* "And not only this, but we also exult in our tribulations, knowing that tribulation brings about perseverance; and perseverance, proven character; and proven character, hope; and hope does not disappoint, because the love of God has been poured out within our hearts through the Holy Spirit who was given to us" (Romans 5:3-5). Although there will be difficult times in our service to God, we can be sure that He will be with us every step of the way. Met with prayer and faith, life's challenges will only strengthen and solidify our relationships with God. Each obstacle overcome leaves us stronger and more prepared for greater service in the kingdom.

• *Delight.* "Trust in the Lord, and do good; Dwell in the land and cultivate faithfulness. Delight yourself in the Lord; And He will give you the desires of your heart. Commit your way to the Lord, Trust also in Him, and He will do it" (Psalm 37:3-5). As Christians, we should experience joy in the journey. We are a blessed people with so much to be grateful for. With happy, contented hearts we will be able to delight in our unique roles in the kingdom.

• *Dedication.* "Who shall separate us from the love of Christ? Shall tribulation, or distress, or persecution, or famine, or nakedness, or peril, or sword? Just as it is written, 'For Thy sake we are being put to death all day long; We were considered as sheep to be slaughtered.' But in all these things we overwhelmingly conquer through Him who loved us" (Romans 8:35-37). With our eyes fixed on God and our feet rooted in His Word, our commitment to the cause of Christ will help us give our all. If He is first in our hearts, our lives will bear witness to our devotion. Dedicated to our Lord, nothing will draw us away from His love and mercy.

• *Dependence.* "Trust in the Lord with all your heart, And do not lean on your own understanding. In all your ways acknowledge Him, And He will make your paths straight" (Proverbs 3:5-6). The most important aspect of giving heart, soul and might to God is realizing our dependence on Him. Pride can tempt even the most righteous, sincere Christian into putting her own ideas before God's. We must remember that God is our Creator, Sustainer and Savior. Without Him, we are nothing; with Him, our lives can be filled with joy and blessings beyond description. If we give God our humble, willing spirits, our lives will be transformed for His glory.

For What It's Worth

What a friend we have in Mary, the mother of our Lord. Her story of faith begins with the angel's stunning announcement that she, a virgin, would conceive and give birth to the Son of God. Her commitment to God carried her through Jesus' earthly ministry, to His death on the cross, and finally, to His triumphal resurrection and ascension. Her willingness to serve God dramatically altered the course she had set for her life, yet she humbly assumed her role in God's plan. She served God thankfully in the role He gave her. We, too, should strive to serve daily in our unique spheres of influence. God deserves nothing less than our best, which means sacrificing our will to Him. This kind of commitment implies love, devotion and trust. Truly giving ourselves to God means giving the total of our being: heart, soul, strength and mind.

Give an Answer

1. How did Mary respond to the news that she would conceive and give birth to the Son of God (Luke 1:26-27, 46-55)?

2. Explain Simeon's message to Mary in the temple (Luke 2:29-35). Recall times in Jesus' life when she probably reflected on those words.

3. Relate the events that took place at the wedding in Cana of Galilee. What can we learn about Mary from the events described in John 2:1-11?

4. How did Jesus display His love and appreciation for Mary while on the cross (John 19:26-27)?

5. Read the first two chapters of Acts. Assuming Mary stayed with the disciples until the Day of Pentecost, how do you think she was impacted by the events described in 2:41-47?

6. Record scriptures that shed light on how we are to serve God with all our hearts, souls and might.

Give It Some Thought

1. How would you describe Mary, as viewed through Scripture? How does her story touch you?

2. Why is it significant to realize that Mary simply served God in

the role He gave her? What application can we make to our own lives from this observation?

3. List qualities that are necessary for giving ourselves fully to God. Why is our attitude important to our effectiveness in His kingdom?

4. Discuss some of the difficulties of serving God with all your heart, soul and might. How can we remain faithful and focused through life's challenges?

5. Can you think of Christian women like Mary who serve faithfully in their unique spheres of influence?

Give It a Try

1. Are you letting your light shine in your unique sphere of influence? On a sheet of paper, write your name in the middle. Around it, write other people's names with whom your life intersects. Begin praying that you can be an example to these people and look for opportunities to minister to them.

2. Each of us has a special role in the kingdom of God, as individual as we are. Examine your responsibilities in this stage of life. Are you serving God with all of your heart, soul and might? Are there areas where you need to make changes in order to please God, or are there aspects of your life that you need to embrace as part of the unique purpose He has given you?

3. Write a letter to a Christian sister you admire for serving with faithfulness, humility and enthusiasm.

CHAPTER 13

THE GIVER
OF GOOD GIFTS

"Every good thing bestowed and every perfect gift is from above, coming down from the Father of lights, with whom there is no varia- tion, or shifting shadow" (James 1:17).

During this study, we have examined the grace of giving. Along the way, we have encountered many women of the Bible whose stories of generosity and faith model unique ways we can honor our Lord through our eagerness to give. Their examples powerfully demonstrate the impact one person can have for the kingdom of God. These biblical characters served God in amazing ways, and their stories inspire us to live with greater compassion and humility. As inspiring as these women of the Bible are, however, we will miss the full scope of our charge to give if we leave this study without looking at the One whom we serve when we give.

"Come and see the works of God, Who is awesome in His deeds toward the sons of men," Psalm 66:5 urges. God is truly the giver of good gifts. He has done so much for us, both individually and as a people. First, He created our world with all its beauty and splendor. God's revealed Word begins with this fact: "In the beginning God created the heavens and the earth" (Genesis 1:1). The sights, sounds and smells of nature work together to remind us of the earth's masterful design. A morning walk through a flower-strewn field of dewy grass when all is quiet; a leisurely afternoon spent picnicking on a mountaintop while clouds billow overhead; or an evening spent on the beach under a canopy of stars – all allow us to see the fingerprints of God on our world.

Our great and perfect God also gives us unconditional love. Romans 8:38-39 boldly declares,

> For I am convinced that neither death, nor life, nor angels, nor principalities, nor things present, nor things to come, nor powers, nor height, nor depth, nor any other created thing, shall be able to separate us from the love of God, which is in Christ Jesus our Lord.

Although we are unworthy of His compassion or mercy, God's love is steady and faithful. In fact, He cares more for our physical and spiritual well-being than we do. No matter how far we stray from the path of righteousness, we can never wander so far as to escape our Father's love.

God's love for His children is displayed in many ways, but His greatest gift to mankind is this: "For God so loved the world, that He gave His only begotten Son, that whoever believes in Him should not perish, but have eternal life" (John 3:16). Because of God's willingness to sacrifice His Son and because of Jesus' willingness to leave the glories of heaven to endure indescribable suffering, we have been redeemed. We have hope of eternal life because we were purchased with the blood of Christ.

Because of Christ's willingness to give Himself up for us, we have a plan of salvation and freedom from the chains of sin and death. In Him, we have a faithful Friend and an intercessor with the Father. We also have God's will revealed in Scripture and His love displayed through the body of Christ, the church.

Besides the gifts given to us as a people, God blesses each of us individually. Romans 8:32 asks, "He who did not spare His own Son, but delivered Him up for us all, how will He not also with Him freely give us all things?" If God could make the ultimate sacrifice in sending His perfect Son to die for sinful people who were unworthy and ungrateful, how much more do you think He desires to heap blessings upon His children? Like a kind and loving Father, God desires to give us our hearts' desires. Matthew 7:11 reminds us, "If you then, being evil, know how to give good gifts to your children, how much more shall your Father who is in heaven give what is good to those who ask Him!"

Indeed, each of us is blessed beyond what we could ever ask for or deserve. The hymn "Father of Mercies" says,

> Father of mercies, day by day
> My love to Thee grows more and more;
> Thy gifts are strewn upon my way
> Like sands upon the great seashore ... .

God's boundless, matchless love is revealed to each of us through His tender care, physical blessings and abiding presence.

When Opportunity Knocks

Considering all that God has done for us, He asks so little in return. We demonstrate our thanksgiving to God when we cheerfully use our resources to help others. Hebrews 13:16 says, "And do not neglect doing good and sharing; for with such sacrifices God is pleased." Our blessings do bring with them responsibility; and to whom much has been given, much is expected. Our duty to share our blessings is best summed up with Matthew 10:8's simple reminder, "freely you received, freely give."

We have countless opportunities to give each day. Being alert will help us seize more of these opportunities, so that we may excel in the art of giving. As we move through our days, our lives intersect with many others. If we are attentive and compassionate, we will find many more possibilities for service in these encounters. Listed here are some of those who will be blessed by our commitment to give.

• *God.* God has given us so much. For Who He is, He deserves our love, trust and devotion. For all He has done for us, He deserves glory, honor and gratitude. When we give God our time and resources, He will give us so much more in return. And when we serve the people around us, He says we are really ministering to Him (Matthew 25:37-40).

• *Church.* As the body of Christ, each member's contributions are vital to the proper functioning and growth of the church. As we give our time to worship and Bible study, we will be edified and strengthened in our faith. Sharing our resources and abilities will help us further the gospel and minister to those in need.

• *Loved Ones.* Like the virtuous woman in Proverbs 31, we should not look past those closest to us when considering whom we should serve. We have great potential to influence our loved ones. Freely sharing with them our time, love, humor and wisdom will result in spiritually nourishing relationships that will be counted among our greatest treasures in life.

• *Fellow Christians.* God's design for the church demonstrates His tender care for His children. As brothers and sisters in Christ, we may support and encourage each other as we strive to live according to God's Word. Being devoted to and preferring fellow Christians, as Romans 12:10 urges, means maintaining an active posture in regard to our brothers and sisters. Keeping our eyes open to unmet needs and making time for fellowship will help us cultivate stronger relationships. As fellow heirs of grace, our burdens will be lighter and our path will be brighter as we journey together.

• *Strangers.* "Do not neglect to show hospitality to strangers, for by this some have entertained angels without knowing it" (Hebrews 13:2). Even in our briefest, most anonymous encounters, we can let our lights shine. We must remember that each person we meet is a precious soul created by God. Whether in line at the grocery store check-out, in the stands at a sporting event, or on the phone with a telemarketer, we should treat all people with kindness, gentleness and respect. We cannot fully know the struggles or unmet needs of individuals we meet as we go through the day – or how much a kind word, listening ear or thoughtful deed might mean. Even the smallest gesture might plant a seed for developing a friendship or for sharing the gospel.

• *Enemies.* "But love your enemies, and do good, and lend, expecting nothing in return; and your reward will be great, and you will be sons of the Most High; for He Himself is kind to ungrateful and evil men" (Luke 6:35). When trying to picture our enemies, we might draw a blank. For me, the word "enemy" conjures images of an evil, masked villain cloaked in black. Thankfully, most of us don't have soap-opera-worthy arch enemies who seek at every turn to ruin our lives. From time to time, however, we probably all will encounter people who will snub or belittle us, treat us rudely or hurt our feelings in one way or another. Other times, even in the church, we may interact with people whose personalities annoy or offend us. Rather than lashing out in anger or avoiding these people altogether, 1 Peter 3:8-9 urges,

> To sum up, let all be harmonious, sympathetic, brotherly, kindhearted, and humble in spirit; not returning evil for evil, or insult for insult, but giving a blessing instead; for you were called for the very purpose that you might inherit a blessing.

There is such truth in Christ's statement, "It is more blessed to give than to receive" (Acts 20:35). When we are generous with the blessings entrusted to us, we honor God and experience the joy of serving others. And our giving will not be overlooked by our Lord, who will notice and reward our good deeds:

> Give, and it will be given to you; good measure, pressed down, shaken together, running over, they will pour into your lap. For by your standard of measure it will be measured to you in return (Luke 6:38).

God's Giving Women

All of us have the means to give if we are willing. During our study we have met many amazing, inspiring women who model generosity and compassion. Before we close, let us look briefly at the women of the Bible we have studied and the special lessons each has taught us.

• *With All of Her Mite.* With only two mites, the widow described in Luke 21:2-4 has taught more about giving money than anyone else in history. She gave all that she had with an attitude of humility and thankfulness. Her example is so poignant because she did not give of her abundance but of her poverty. This shows us that rich or poor, all can give. All that we have belongs to God; we are merely stewards of what is already His. Keeping that in mind, we will be able to give of our material blessings in a way that meets needs and glorifies our Father.

• *Talents to Share.* Dorcas, whom we meet in Acts 9:36-42, used her sewing abilities to clothe the widowed and the poor. We, too, may use our God-given gifts to bless others and glorify our Lord. We must evaluate our unique abilities, work to develop them, and seek opportunities to use them. If we are willing to offer our hearts and hands in service to God, then, like Dorcas, we can be vessels of the love of God.

• *Welcome Home.* Acts 16:14-40 invites us to meet Lydia. After she was converted by Paul, she opened her home to the apostles. After Paul and Silas were imprisoned, her home became a haven for her fellow Christians and a place of refuge for two weary, mistreated prisoners. Like Lydia, we can impact the kingdom of God by extending our hands in friendship and hospitality. Scripture encourages us to reach out to fellow Christians, strangers and souls in need. If we take seriously God's command to practice hospitality, we will minister to lost souls, encourage the saints, and develop friendships that will sustain us throughout life.

• *Ready to Serve.* In the story of the unnamed woman of Luke 7:36-50, we see a poignant example of humility and courage intertwined. In the home of Simon the Pharisee, she kissed Jesus' feet, washed them with her tears, anointed them with oil, and dried them with her hair. When we are able to empty ourselves of vanity, pride and selfishness, we too will be able to give ourselves to God in acts of service. If we recognize ourselves as slaves of Christ, we can meekly follow His example of washing people's feet. Doing so, we will fulfill Christ's definition of leadership through servanthood.

• *Treasures of the Heart.* First Samuel 1-2:21 shares the story of Hannah. Barren for many years, Hannah pleaded for a son and promised to dedicate him to God. Hannah honored this promise with a beautiful prayer of thanksgiving. Like Hannah, we should love the Lord more than all else that we hold dear. When we give sacrificially, we demonstrate trust in God and acknowledge that our blessings come from Him. True sacrifice is only possible when we realize that our real treasures are being laid up in heaven. When we are willing to sacrifice our earthly treasures, we will please our Father, and the joys of heaven will be ours.

• *An Investment of Time.* While Jesus was a guest in the home of Mary and Martha in Luke 10:38-42, Martha was preoccupied with her chores but Mary sat at His feet. Mary took time to simply experience God and bask in His presence. Like Mary, we must strive daily to keep our priorities in check. Throughout life, our commitment to give our time to God will be challenged. We must remember that although our days are numbered in this life, the Christian is not bound by the world's time. Life is fleeting, but God's time is eternal. When we give God our time, we will be fruitful and blessed in our walk with the Lord.

• *That's What Friends Are For.* Far from the strained, competitive relationships typically expected between mother- and daughter-in-law, Naomi and Ruth give us a powerful example of loyalty and friendship. Their lives are chronicled in the book of Ruth. The first commandment for each of us is to love God with all our hearts, minds and strength; the second is to love our neighbors as ourselves. Our loyalty to God and our friendships with fellow Christians are truly the best gifts we can give ourselves. God will reward our faithfulness to Him, and we will be encouraged and strengthened by relationships cultivated with fellow Christians.

• *The Gift of Knowledge.* Priscilla and Aquila's commitment to teach Apollos in Acts 18:24-28 did more to spread the gospel than they ever could have imagined. Centuries after she lived, Priscilla is still teaching us today. We must also learn to share our faith in a way that is bold, yet gentle. Opportunities abound to share the love of Christ if we are willing. Opening our eyes to teachable moments will allow us to minister powerfully to the people in our lives. Through Bible study, we increase our knowledge and holiness; through teaching we help other people come to know the love of our Father. Through this means of giving, we can plant seeds that, with God's blessing, will bring about spiritual growth today and a glorious harvest in eternity.

• *Giving to Meet Urgent Needs.* Whenever God asks us to give, we can trust that He will supply the means to give. In 1 Kings 17, the widow of Zarephath responded to God's call by sharing her food and water with Elijah. She learned that when we open our hands and let go of what we have, the Lord heaps blessings upon us. She serves as an example for us today because of her willingness to sacrifice to meet urgent needs and to give beyond what was required. We, too, have opportunities to give when the Lord calls. Ultimately, our good deeds will demonstrate the love of Christ, bringing honor and glory to our Lord.

• *Anna and the King.* Anna, whom we read about in Luke 2:36-

38, devoted her life to worshiping God. Because she was so devout, she was able to see Jesus and prophesy about Him to all who
were eagerly awaiting the Messiah. We should also keep the Lord
at the center of our lives. Through Bible study, prayer and praise,
we sharpen our spiritual focus and renew our minds. Beyond this,
bringing God into our relationships with other people will give
these relationships new depth. We also have the privilege of coming together as a church family. When we worship God, we become
a little more empty of ourselves and a little more full of Him. This
is the best gift we can give our Father.

  • *Take My Life.* What an example and friend we have in Mary,
the mother of our Lord. Her story of faith begins in Luke 1 and is
woven throughout the Gospels. She served God willingly and thankfully in the role He gave her. God gives each of us a unique role to
play in the kingdom. He deserves nothing less than our best, giv-
en with love, devotion and trust.

  As we leave this study, let us not simply close this book and allow these new friends to recede quietly into the shadows of our
minds. Instead, try to remember these women of the Bible and accept the unique challenges that each one offers. Rather than letting their examples fade, let us seek to carry on their legacies of
faith in our lives today. And let us strive to weave their finest qualities into our own lives – taking a bit of strength, courage, humility or compassion from each one.

  Just as the women we have studied inspire us to give, let us spur
each other on to greater levels of service in our Christian walk. First
Corinthians 12:18 says, "But now God has placed the members,
each one of them, in the body, just as He desired." Each one of us
has an individual and special role in the kingdom of God. As parts
of the body of Christ, we should value and celebrate each member's
contributions. Let us look for the goodness in our sisters in Christ
– cheering each other's spiritual victories and offering motivation
when we fall short. We close our study with Colossians 1:9-12. As
we offer each other support and encouragement, may the tender
words of this passage be written on our hearts:

> For this reason also, since the day we heard of it, we
> have not ceased to pray for you and to ask that you may
> be filled with the knowledge of His will in all spiritual

wisdom and understanding, so that you may walk in a manner worthy of the Lord, to please Him in all respects, bearing fruit in every good work and increasing in the knowledge of God; strengthened with all power, according to His glorious might, for the attaining of all steadfastness and patience; joyously giving thanks to the Father, who has qualified us to share in the inheritance of the saints in light.

For What It's Worth

We opened our study with a story about little Bridgette. When told by her mother that it was time to give her money to God, a perplexed Bridgette looked around and asked, "Which one is He?" Her innocent question is best answered by our Lord, who told His followers in Matthew 25:40 that when we give to others, we are really ministering to Him: "Truly I say to you, to the extent that you did it to one of these brothers of Mine, even the least of them, you did it to Me." When we share our time and resources as we have opportunity – with the church, our loved ones, fellow Christians, strangers or enemies – we honor and glorify God. He has given us so much more than we could ever ask for or deserve, but our blessings bring responsibility to share.

There are many ways that we can give. During our study, we have encountered many women of the Bible who gave in unique ways. Their stories set powerful examples for us to emulate today. As we leave this study, let us strive daily to give all we can. If we desire to serve God with pure and humble hearts, we can trust that our Lord will always supply the means to give.

Give an Answer

1. Read and explain Romans 1:20.
2. What can separate us from the love of God, according to Romans 8:38-39?
3. What can we learn about God's unconditional love from the parable of the prodigal son in Luke 15:11-32?
4. Read Ephesians 1:3-14. List the blessings noted in this beautiful passage.

5. Of what are we assured in Matthew 7:9-11?

6. What has God given us, according to Ephesians 2:4-10? How is He described in this passage?

Give It Some Thought

1. What can we give to God? How does our willingness to give demonstrate thankfulness for all He has done for us?

2. "The church hasn't done anything for me," we might hear someone complain. Why is a me-first attitude detrimental to the body of Christ? How can we focus on serving rather than being served?

3. What do our loved ones and fellow Christians need from us? What potential do these relationships have to bless us?

4. How will focusing on our roles as ambassadors for Christ affect our interaction with strangers?

5. Why is 1 Peter 3:8-9 difficult to put into practice? How can kindness diffuse a tense situation? Can you recall a time when you responded gently to someone who was unkind to you?

Give It a Try

1. To become more keenly aware of the unique blessings God has given you, begin a gratitude journal. You might aspire to note a single blessing each day or plan to use your journal to pen deeply personal letters of thanksgiving to God.

2. Look back at the list of those who will be blessed by your commitment to give, and brainstorm ways you could give more.

3. List all the women of the Bible whose lives we have studied. For each character, note a new insight you have gained and a personal challenge you take from her story of generosity.